THE TECHNIQUES OF DELEGATING

THE TECHNIQUES OF DELEGATING

How to Get Things Done through Others

By DONALD A. LAIRD and ELEANOR C. LAIRD

McGRAW-HILL BOOK COMPANY, INC.

NEW YORK   TORONTO   LONDON

THE TECHNIQUES OF DELEGATING

Library of Congress Catalog Card Number: 57–11861

FIRST EDITION

PUBLISHED BY THE McGRAW-HILL BOOK COMPANY, INC.

PREFACE

Delegating has been dealt with in the past as if it were as mechanical or logical a process as routing the flow of work. But many recent psychological investigations of on-going establishments have indicated that delegating involves much more than a logically constructed organization chart. Human or psychological factors have to be considered, as well as logical and economical factors.

This book, which we believe is the first to be devoted primarily to delegating, calls attention to the psychological factors. We have recast some of the older theories about delegating to be more in accord with the psychological and social forces which have been found to affect group activities.

This book is titled "The Techniques of," rather than "The Psychology of," for two reasons. For one, the book emphasizes the practical. In addition, the present state of knowledge about delegating is incomplete, making it impossible to outline a psychology of delegating to which most specialists in industrial psychology and group dynamics would agree. For such specialists, this book should suggest research problems that need investigation.

This book was written primarily for the busy—perhaps too busy—practical man of affairs. Partly because of the state of knowledge, we have drawn about as heavily from successful executives' and administrators' methods as we have from psychological research and social theory. It has also seemed desirable at times to report the unsuccessful executives' methods. We hope this treatment will stimulate thinking as well as supply some "rules for delegating" which appear to be substantiated.

Although this book is written in the idiom with which the business person is familiar, we have been mindful of the needs of the teacher of business courses. We have tried to set up a framework and give examples which will provide these instructors with ammunition that will enable them to devote more class time to the practical psychology of delegating. The book may also serve as collateral reading for their students as well as in company-sponsored executive training courses.

Our profound thanks go to John Moriarty and the staff of the Purdue University Libraries, to Nevin W. Raber and the staff of the business branch of the Indianapolis Public Library, and to Louise Lage and the staff of the library of Eli Lilly and Company. All these cooperated in generously making their facilities available to us.

We are also indebted to the following, who read various portions of this book to check our interpretations and simplifications of their findings, or to quote from their writings: Earl Brooks, Edwin A. Fleishman, Frederick J. Gaudet, John H. Gorsuch, D. Hastie, John K. Hemphill, H. B. Kiphuth, Charles L. Lapp, Myles L. Mace, A. J. Pastene, Lyle M. Spencer, Charles R. Walker, Robert G. Williamson, and W. F. Wrightnour.

DONALD A. LAIRD
ELEANOR C. LAIRD

CONTENTS

THE TECHNIQUES OF DELEGATING

1
GETTING THINGS DONE THROUGH OTHERS

The new automobile owners

"There aren't enough hours in the day."

"I wish I were twins so I could get caught up."

"The company should give me more assistants."

"No matter how furiously I work, I am still snowed under."

It is the aim of this book to point out ways to get caught up, and stay caught up, by working through others. Delegating is the usual word for it. The backbone of modern big business, it is also helpful in small business, and for individuals, as the following examples show [11, 78].*

* The numbers in brackets refer to recommended readings, or research sources which bear on the topic of a paragraph, or of a section. The readings and sources are listed at the back of the book.

Two small-town druggists bought automobiles from the same dealer during the same week. Both were cash sales, but there was the red tape of transferring titles, changing registrations and insurance.

The aggressive druggist with the wire-brush mustache insisted upon looking after those unfamiliar details himself. He tilted his head to read the fine print on the blanks and snorted about all the bother. He had to make two trips to the courthouse, one to his insurance agency, and an extra trip back to the dealer to check on a serial number. It took him a half day and left him weary and in too poor a humor to enjoy his new car that day.

The other druggist, with the porcupine-style haircut, delegated all the red-tape details. Instead of stumbling and grumbling through the courthouse maze, he took his wife for a ride in the country.

"You folks know all about changing the title and such," he had told the dealer as he jingled the car keys. "Show me where to sign the blanks, and you can mail the papers to me when they are completed. And since your office girl has all the numbers, she might call the Jones Agency and tell them to shift my policy to the new car."

It took the second druggist less than two minutes to delegate to people who knew how to look after the details. Failing to delegate used a half day of the first druggist's time, and made more work and bother for everyone concerned.

Saving one's own time is often a person's chief reason for delegating. But these druggists highlight two other advantages that accrue from handing the details over to people with more know-how: (*a*) other people's time is saved, and (*b*) the job is usually done better [25].

The two teachers

Delegating also changes a one-person activity into a working organization, as the teachers' story illustrates. Both were young, conscientious, and with little experience in the classroom.

The one who favored plain dresses kept herself busy all day in a marathon race in the classroom. She passed out supplies, collected papers, cleaned blackboards, tried to maintain discipline, tried to teach. The details kept her so chained to the job that she had to wait until evenings to grade papers. She complained that teaching was hard work, took long hours, and that it was making her jumpy.

The other teacher, who liked to wear frilly dresses, delegated many of the classroom details to the pupils themselves. Handing out supplies and cleaning the blackboards were easily delegated to the pupils. The pupils enjoyed having these responsibilities given them.

The tallest boy, who had failed to pass two grades, washed the tops of the blackboards. His pride in this responsibility helped keep him from being the trouble-maker he had been for previous teachers. (In Chapter 12 we will learn about using delegation to help with similar problem cases in business.)

Each morning the teacher with the frilly dress wrote the day's delegations on a corner of the blackboard. She carefully rotated the tasks—except for cleaning the tops of the blackboards—so that each pupil had a turn at something he could accomplish with least supervision. Partiality was kept at a low point.

This second teacher had something more than a room of pupils to teach. Her planned delegation transformed the pupils into an organization that got things done for the group.

The first teacher was trying to run a one-person enterprise, and was not making good. The second was administering an organized enterprise she had created by delegating, and she did not have to take work home.

The modern ailment called "briefcaseitis"—lugging work home evenings to get caught up on the job—is often caused by not delegating various responsibilities from one's job. About 50 per cent of executives and professional workers have this ailment [100, 108].

The two physicians

Two young physicians who had interned together compared experiences and held a "business clinic" after they had been in general practice a few years. Each bragged a little about being kept busy every minute. Each charged the same rates for calls and treatments.

But it turned out that one was taking in almost half again as much money as the other. How could this happen when they charged the same fees and were working equally long hours? The answer: one delegated more than the other.

Each employed a recent high school graduate as office girl. One physician used his girl mostly to answer the telephone when he was away from the office. When he was in the office, he would interrupt examining a patient to answer the telephone himself. He collected fees personally and kept his own books.

His office girl was not much assistance to this stockily built physician. And he was doing nothing that might help make her more useful. His patients grumbled a bit about their long waits in his correctly named "waiting room," while the office girl worked at crossword puzzles.

But the tall, slender physician was rendering his office girl more valuable each week. He was training her continually and delegating more details to her as part of this training. Right from the start he let her handle all telephone calls. If she couldn't handle one while he was with a patient, she would have him call back as soon as he had a break in time between patients. No interrupted examinations.

From the start he asked her to open and sort his mail. Soon he showed her how to sort invoices and check them. She wrote out the checks for him to sign. He trained her to sterilize instruments and to make some routine chemical analyses. She kept his books and got information together at the year's end for his income tax computations.

The tall, slender physician could thus spend a larger share of his time on the essentials of his profession. He could examine and treat about 50 per cent more patients a day than the other physician, and without working harder. He had time left over to study up on new developments in medicine. And his girl found her work much more interesting than the one who devoted most of her on-the-job time to puzzles and personal telephone calls which kept the line busy when some patients were in a hurry to get a call through.

As with the school teacher who liked frilly dresses, the tall physician delegated to people who were less capable than he. But he delegated by easy stages, so that gradually the other person became more capable. Everybody concerned was a gainer from this.

Sometimes we hear a person say that he dare not delegate because he has no one working for him who is capable enough to take over the duty. Such a statement may be an indirect confession that he has not been delegating in ways that would steadily make his associates more capable [25].

The two mothers

"How do you manage to hold down a job and also take care of all these children?" Chicago reporters asked a thirty-nine-year-old working woman who had just given birth to her nineteenth child.

"We manage just fine," she smiled back. "We all have our share of work, even the one-and-a-half-year-old. He moves the chairs so the others can sweep."

The sheer size of the family forced delegating on her.

Contrast her with the well-to-do mother of two daughters. This one made mothering a full-time job. She even mothered her general-purpose maid; but the maids called it too-much-bossing, and seldom stayed longer than a month.

This well-to-do mother insisted upon dressing her daughters long after they were able to, and keenly wanted to, dress themselves. "They look so much neater," mother said, "when I dress them."

As they grew up, the well-to-do mother decided most

things for her daughters, because "mother knows best." She usually put her knuckles firmly on her hips when she said that to them.

She still planned and personally bought their clothes until they married. When they left home, neither daughter knew how to keep house or prepare a meal.

But we can be pretty certain that those nineteen children in Chicago could keep house, cook, and take care of babies when they were married. Delegating in the home had prepared them for a practical life.

Excessive mothering, such as the well-to-do lady indulged in, has been called "smothering." It smothers initiative and often generates resentment. It is not confined to family life, either [86].

Sometimes an employer in effect smothers his employees by doing all the thinking for them. This sort may pass along job details he does not like to do himself, but he rarely actually delegates. His methods are arbitrary or restrictive, in contrast with permissive procedures. The restrictive smothering takes more of the employer's time in the long run, and does not create an organization that will pull together to get things done.

Smothering, or bossiness, makes the other person dependent. Almost always it puts his initiative in cold storage, although it may crop out in resentment or grumbling. But real delegating enables the other person to stand on his own feet. He does not have to "run to papa for help." He is also less inclined to complain about papa to his playmates.

Some firms, such as Sears, Roebuck and Company, intentionally give their key people such a large number of people to supervise that it is not possible to boss closely. The old theory that the span of control should be limited to about seven workers made it too easy for a domineering key person to be too restrictive for efficient delegating [27].

The foremen

One of the best examples of what delegating can do was uncovered in an analysis of an automobile assembly line. This was observed in a modern new factory by Dr. Charles R. Walker and colleagues from the Yale Institute of Human Relations [106].

The foremen were kept on the jump every minute and had to be cast-iron men. During a work day the typical foreman was occupied with some six hundred separate and distinct incidents on which he had to take some action. That averaged less than a minute per action. There was scant time to think or plan, because another interruption, or action, was a few seconds away.

Some of the foremen grunted that their jobs were just one explosion after another—a never-ending string of quick decisions.

Although industrial engineers had set up the foremen's jobs so that no one job would be more demanding than another, there was an obvious difference in the job pressure on different foremen. Some of the foremen did not have as many explosions to take care of.

This was because a few of the foremen had informally delegated parts of their jobs to various men in their sections of the assembly line. It was mostly the more experienced, or the more successful foremen, who had done this. The foremen who delegated to the workers were running their jobs. The foremen who did not delegate were being run ragged by the same jobs.

A swarthy foreman gives us an example of those who were running their jobs. Although he was one of the youngest and least experienced, he was making good use of delegation. He had asked various workers to watch for some of the minor explosions, to prevent the explosion, or at least to take care of it if it did happen.

Some of his assemblers were watching for "dings" (dents) as cars came along the line. When they spotted a ding, they told the utility man—not the foreman—about it so the utility man could straighten it out before the car came to the end of the line.

Other workers were delegated to keep an eye on supplies of subassemblies which fed into the line and to follow through when a supply thinned out. Another was delegated to look after the jigs and fixtures, preventing breakdowns before they exploded.

In addition, every worker on his part of the line was delegated to watch for imperfections from work ahead of him on the line and to make corrections whenever possible. Fewer cars were shunted to the side on final inspection as a result of this delegation. It also probably made the routine assembly tasks more interesting and more challenging to the workers; they were making minor decisions in addition to bolting and clipping parts together. It broadened their jobs and gave their routine chores more meaning.

But many of the other foremen tried to look after all such details themselves. As a consequence, they were "carrying too much sail."

This swarthy young foreman had built an organization in his section of the line. The organization took care of

(From the booklet "The Worry-Go-Round." Courtesy of the Connecticut Mutual Life Insurance Co.)

Many jobs are a series of explosions until some details and decision making are delegated.

many of the sails for him. This cut down the hundreds of daily interruptions he would have had without such delegating.

The supervisors who neglected to delegate were as good as chained to the line. They hesitated to go to the washroom, lest all doom break out with no one experienced to handle it.

But the swarthy foreman could spend a third of the day away from his department or in uninterrupted planning. He always let his senior utility man know where he could be found, however, just in case something happened that his informal organization could not cope with.

Delegating put him on top of his job. We daresay it made him promotable, too.

There is much more to delegating than merely telling another to do something for us. It was imposing, not delegating, when the old lady who lived at the bus turnaround gave the driver her shopping list and instructed him just where to buy the items for her.

The highest form of delegating is when some of the decision making that affects the man's job is passed along to the man concerned. That is what the swarthy foreman did. Here are some of the things it accomplished:

1. Eased the job pressure on him
2. Developed assistants who were capable of acting on their own in minor emergencies
3. Provided for his absence or for periods of uninterrupted thinking and planning
4. Made the routine jobs more satisfying to the workers
5. Improved the quality of the product
6. Gave his workers some group goals which made them more of a team

Which of those six would have been achieved if he had delegated only the errand running and the job details he did not enjoy? Or if he had smothered his workers by keeping close watch on each detail after he had handed it over to them?

"The best executive," Theodore Roosevelt observed, "is the one who has sense enough to pick good men to do what he wants done, and self-restraint enough to keep from meddling with them while they do it."

The good executives are not all in offices and factories. Some of them are in kitchens and schoolrooms and churches. They use delegation to build an organization that will get things done through others. This sounds easy to do, as the old lady at the bus turnaround imagined. But there are many ins and outs to doing it successfully. This book is about those ins and outs.

In the next chapter we will begin to track down some of these, and to discover what they have contributed to the success of some outstanding businessmen. Whether big business, or small business, or just the business of family life, the principles we will uncover are much the same [11].

It is well to be familiar with the principles and the ins and outs before attempting to delegate. The impulse to jump right in and start delegating should be restrained until this book has been digested, so that thoughtful plans can be worked out which will more likely make the delegating a success from the start.

2

**SOME
PSYCHOLOGICAL
ASPECTS OF
DELEGATING**

Andrew Carnegie's open secret

Delegating seems simple: just decide what someone else could do to make the job easier for you, then tell him to do it. But parents often find that it is not that simple when they tell their children to wash the dishes.

Delegating is a complicated process . . . because it involves the relationships between the most sensitive machines in the world—people, and also because of two almost contradictory tendencies which are looked upon as characteristics of our Western civilization of today: (*a*) From infancy we have been trained to look toward some more powerful or more capable person for leadership and making important decisions. (*b*) But we also want our individual dignity to be esteemed by others; to have our wishes and welfare given prime consideration when decisions are made, or to take part ourselves in reaching those decisions which affect us—the theme of modern democracy.

Old-fashioned delegating overlooked the second part. Modern delegating not only shares the work details, but also passes along much of the decision making which affects those work details. Modern delegating is not just getting others to help out on our jobs, but also giving them the authority and freedom to handle the details on their own initiative.

When industrial development started, only a little more than a century ago, the men of action and ingenious mechanics who started their own small factories usually overlooked delegating. Some of those early enterprises were so small, the owners were not pressed to delegate. The business could keep going because the owner worked harder and longer. But if the enterprise started to grow, then the owner was forced to delegate. Often he delegated to a relative.

Andrew Carnegie, shortly before the turn of this century, was one of the first to make large-scale use of delegation as it is now conceived. He had no children to whom he could delegate power and authority. His few relatives were given comfortable jobs, but Carnegie delegated mostly to capable people who were not relatives. He picked "the best man," let this man have his own way in doing the jobs delegated to him, and checked on the results.

Canny Andy, as he was called behind his back, delegated vigorously to build an organization that could grow and expand. Other steel-mill owners who looked after everything themselves ran furiously on treadmills that led nowhere, and they did not dare take their eyes off the job. But Carnegie had time to travel, scheme, and plan some more delegating.

Carnegie made no secret of his use of delegating to get things done through others and to ease the job pressure on himself. In fact, he enjoyed bragging about it:

"It marks a big step in a man's development when he comes to realize that other men can be called in to help him do a better job than he can do alone." (He made that big step early in his business life.)

"Take away our factories, but leave me my organization, and in four years I will have re-established myself." (That from the man who seriously thought of retiring when he was thirty.)

"The man isn't worth his salt who cannot have his affairs so efficiently organized that he can drop them at a moment's notice." (He paid one man the fabulous salary of a million dollars a year; he put big money into organizing his affairs.)

"The secret of success is not in doing your own work, but in recognizing the right man to do it." (His mills produced as much steel as the whole of England.)

He even proposed an epitaph for his gravestone which praised delegating: "Here lies a man who knew how to enlist in his service better men than himself." (Such flattery for his delegatees quite likely stimulated them, for here was a leader who passed along praise and credit as well as fabulous salaries.)

Such public comments, which beaming Carnegie loved to make, and his phenomenal success, probably made other businessmen give some thought to delegating. But many owners were not temperamentally in tune with Carnegie's idea. They just couldn't bring themselves "to abdicate." And today, although top management authorities are loud in urging more delegating, surveys we will review in a later chapter reveal that at least one-third of executives are underdelegating.

Frank Woolworth's breakdown

Some early owners learned about the need for delegating through the "school of experience." Frank W. Woolworth, for example, after several failures, was just turning his five-and-dime-store idea around the corner to success when a nervous breakdown knocked him out. He did not have robust health to begin with, and this breakdown was attributed to overwork.

During his slow recovery he reached a conclusion which he later called his most important discovery: "I lost my conceit that nobody could do anything as well as I could. So long as I had the idea that I must attend personally to everything, large-scale operation was impossible."

The Model-T story

Henry Ford did not put much faith in Carnegie's and Woolworth's teachings about delegating. Automobile maker Ford had strong streaks of secrecy and mistrust which inclined him to hold all the reins in his own hands. He would not give his executives the information they needed to know about the business if they were to make sound decisions. Fate had put him in a rapidly expanding industry, but he had essentially a one-man company, with scant delegation to give it an organization or a nervous system.

Ford's business fell far behind General Motors, which was building an organization as well as automobiles. Alfred P. Sloan, Jr., first as president and then as chairman, spent twenty years establishing delegation as a basic practice in the General Motors enterprises. Meanwhile, Ford remained a one-genius affair: plant acreage grew, but delegating could not take root [24].

At Ford's peak he had 65 per cent of the automobile market. By World War II his share had trickled down to only 20 per cent. Insiders in Detroit are convinced that Ford Motors lost money during the last fifteen years the original owner was running it.

The next chapters of the Ford story are in great contrast. Henry Ford II was only twenty-five when he took over, following the deaths of his father and grandfather. He was acquainted with modern business organization and knew that delegating is the basic tool for operating any enterprise.

Henry II immediately surrounded himself with a few men who had proven their organizing and delegating skills in other firms. Gradually an organization, or nervous system, was developed. Decision making for most operating problems was decentralized (delegated) so that action could be taken when it should be. And the executives who took the actions acted largely upon their own rather than somebody else's decisions. The chains were taken off their initiative.

The transformation of Ford Motors from a slipping company into a growth company is an epic in the use of delegating in modern business. Henry II is responsible for a much bigger business than his grandfather was, and is operating it profitably and democratically. He has farmed out (delegated) responsibilities and the authority to go with them. He is not personally as rushed and overworked as the founder was. Henry II has time to take full part in civic and community responsibilities, without fear that the business may slip while he has his back turned [78].

The modern purposes of delegating

On hasty consideration, delegating might seem to be adding some inefficiency, similar to putting an extra motion or two into a job. It is easy to see that it can ease an executive's load, but will it bear the cost of the extra help that may be needed?

At the turn of the century most people except Carnegie thought that delegating was something executives did when they employed a private secretary or errand boy to do chores for them. Such personal assistants did provide more arms and legs for the work-harassed executive, but they were scarcely any help in his burden of decision making.

The executive who pushed buttons to summon his breathless assistants was not delegating in the modern meaning of the term. He mostly gave his assistants orders. If he had delegated, modern style, he would not have needed to buzz for his assistants; his delegates would be carrying on on their own, allowing him to rest his ulcer. The gist of delegating, modern style, is making an enter-

prise stronger by giving individuals responsibilities which
will develop the human resources in the enterprise. Delegating, modern conception, is not limited to the few top
executives. It spreads to the grass roots of the organization. The errand-boy aspect is minor in the modern conception of delegating. The major aspect is developing
people who can be trusted to make many work decisions
for themselves, so they don't interrupt or overload their
chief for his advice on, or permission for, every move
they make [63].

Modern delegating thus does not mean hiring extra
help, or putting extra motions into jobs. It is largely shifting some of the thinking and responsibilities from the
executive's job and incorporating them into the jobs of his
employees. When done with skill, it is worth far more than
the cost—a conservative statement, because the cost is
usually only the time the executive spends in planning
and following through on the delegating he does.

As one successful president commented, "We can't put
a price tag on delegating; but we do pay plenty when
delegating breaks down."

Delegating changes the relations between leader and followers

The success of modern delegating hinges upon the relationships between leader and followers. These relationships are much different from those that exist when the
executive issues all the orders, does all the decision making, takes the credit for successes, and blames others for
the failures.

The spirit, or atmosphere, or human climate surrounding a work group seems to determine whether or not delegating will work. Although information on this is sketchy, there are convincing records which underline the importance of this human atmosphere—something the old-fashioned "efficiency expert" overlooked [17, 20–21, 36, 59, Chaps. 1, 2, 62].

Some of the best controlled studies on the role of the human climate have been reported by Dr. Nancy C. Morse and associates, from the Survey Research Center at the University of Michigan. One study dealt with the effects of delegating to the rank and file of semiskilled clerks in some offices of one of the world's largest financial institutions. In some offices they delegated even salary decisions to the clerks! This unusual amount of delegating to the grass roots proved much more successful in some offices than in others. The degree of success appeared to depend largely upon the spirit or human climate that the supervisor had unwittingly set up throughout his office force over the years [54, 92, 89].

The records indicate that delegating works most successfully, in general, when the human climate is democratic, permissive, equalitarian, not secretive, not smothering. In such a climate the person delegated to feels that he is an associate rather than a subordinate, and also feels that he is sharing purposes with his chief, not merely going through motions the chief prescribes [60].

General Mills, Inc., always a powerful enterprise but now a growth company, illustrates that. They have expanded from flour milling into breakfast cereals and cake mixes. They have also succeeded in electronics and chemicals, which seem quite unrelated to foods. This expansion has been possible because the company's policies of delegating helped them develop reserves who were capable of operating the decentralized ventures.

At the top of General Mills, Inc., setting the human climate, is president Charles H. Bell. "Basically people are a complicated piece of mechanism," he comments. "We try to attract people with good sensibilities, then create a climate in which they can make the most of their capabilities. They can't do this where one or two make all the decisions."

Management objectives and underlying factors in management behavior

The favorableness of the climate for delegating can be pin-pointed from somewhat different, though overlapping, points of view. Three approaches are currently in vogue:

Management objectives
Underlying factors in the leaders' behavior
Leadership functions

The *management objectives* which are being stressed in actual operations, and which would presumably make a favorable climate for delegating are:

OBJECTIVE	EXAMPLE
1. Communicating	Keeping workers informed
2. Decision making	Having workers take part in discussions on problems affecting their jobs
3. Cooperation	Teamwork, rather than a system of star players or efficiency experts

Underlying factors in leaders' make-ups tend to make an executive emphasize, usually without being aware of it, certain behavior which influences delegating. One executive may have a streak of secrecy which makes it difficult for him to achieve the objective of communicating. Another may incline to do all the decision making himself, because it is just his nature to dominate a situation.

What are the bedrock factors inside leaders? Some one hundred and fifty things which leaders did as they tried to get things done through others were probed to find an answer to this question. These researches were made mostly by Dr. Edwin A. Fleishman and associates, of the Personnel Research Board at Ohio State University [31, 32, 33, 34].

They found that the 150 different techniques used in handling workers were largely the expressions of only four underlying factors or behavior patterns:

FACTOR	EXAMPLES
1. Consideration	"Our boss is careful not to hurt our feelings."
	"He shows he is pleased when I do a good job."
	"He does not insist that everything be done his way."
2. Initiating structure	"He keeps us informed about rules and policies."
	"He stresses that we should keep ahead of other crews."
	"Sometimes he asks us to put up with unpleasant things for the good of the department."
3. Production emphasis	A minor factor, and closely related to Initiating structure.
4. Social sensitivity	A minor factor, and closely related to Consideration.

An individual leader usually tends to be high in one or two of these factors and medium or even low in others. His "style" of handling people, or his philosophy of leadership, reflects the high or low points in these two basic and two minor underlying factors.

Henry Ford, for instance, was probably low in Consideration and Social Sensitivity. Carnegie was probably high in all four factors.

There is strong evidence that the human climate in a particular enterprise is determined largely by the top man's ranking in these four factors. That is probably why the most successful programs to improve delegating have been those which started at the top [50].

Leadership functions

Success in delegating is also affected by the six functions of the leader. These functions have been uncovered by recent researches by industrial psychologists and industrial sociologists. These functions arise from the relationships between leader and followers, and can be summarized as [17, 60]:

1. Set work goals or objectives *with* the group.
2. Help the work group reach those goals.
3. Coordinate the workers with each other.
4. Help individuals to fit into and be accepted by the work group.
5. Working for the success of the group rather than for one's own record.
6. "Human-ness" (Consideration).

Those six functions overlap or are woven into the objectives of Communicating, Decision Making, and Cooperation. The successful performance of those functions also depends upon the leader's underlying factors.

Setting work objectives with the group, for example, probably overlaps the objective of democratic taking part in Decision Making. Helping them reach the objectives overlaps, or depends upon, the underlying amount of Initiating Structure in the leader's behavior. Helping the individual fit into the work group hinges upon Social Sensitivity and Consideration.

We thus see why effective delegating requires more than the following of a few rules on "How to Delegate." The rules have to be adapted to the total situation and to the human climate prevailing in the place. Often the climate has to be changed before the executive can succeed in getting others to help him carry the load. And in many instances the executive has to shift the way underlying factors are expressed in his own managerial behavior [45].

Delegating is not a gadget one can put on top of the desk, wind it up on Monday morning and then forget until the next Monday. It is a pattern of human relationships that is woven into the executive's hour-by-hour activities and decisions.

In the next chapter we will look into some ways the individual leader can find out whether he is delegating enough, or possibly too much.

3

**FINDING
WHERE
DELEGATING
IS NEEDED**

The owner who looked for a psychiatrist

Sometimes an emergency or a rush of business puts a finger on spots where more delegating is needed. But usually the need creeps into the business or the individual. The need creeps so slowly in most instances that the people concerned may overlook the fact that it is lack of delegating that causes their personal or business ineffectiveness.

The plight of the owner-manager of a medium-sized factory illustrates this. His volume had been steadily increasing, and the outlook might have been rosy but for his worry about his four key foremen. They worked overtime every week, and it had been eighteen months since one of them had been able to take a vacation. They had become prisoners on their jobs.

The owner-manager felt that the four men were slipping, or were not husky enough to stand the pace that the production required.

At the eleventh moment he called on a firm of industrial psychologists. He fingered the row of colored pencils in his pocket as he asked, "Do your people have a psychiatrist who could give my foremen some treatment so they can keep going?"

As he explained his problem, it was apparent that the owner, too, was feeling the strain from the increasing pressure of the business. He had reached the limit of what it is possible for one man to do, but hadn't yet realized it.

As with his foremen, the harder he worked after a certain point, the less effective he became. They were all furiously doing things but not getting as much done as all their effort should have accomplished.

It was obvious—to an outsider—that arrangements were needed to delegate many of the details which had been snowballing the jobs. They didn't need a psychiatrist.

The owner admitted that his own job had been snowballing. It had not occurred to him to delegate; he simply worked faster and longer. Each morning he still checked through the incoming mail. If he didn't answer a letter himself, he penciled detailed instructions (with an indelible pencil) about the answer that should be written by the department concerned.

"Sorting the mail keeps me in touch with the business," he explained. But this chore was taking him twice as long as it had a year before. This was typical of the way neglecting to delegate was creating a rat race for him. It was also setting an example (Initiating structure), so that his key people were afraid to delegate for themselves.

"Those instructions I write on the bottom of the letters —that's delegating, isn't it?" he said a bit wistfully. It was far from delegating, because the owner was the one who had made the decisions. His so-called service manager, for example, was merely carrying out the boss's orders when he replied as per the indelible instructions.

The actions that eased the burdens

The owner's private secretary was that in name only. She was capable of sorting, routing, and answering 90 per cent of the incoming mail without any penciled advice. After this was called to his attention, it took several weeks for him to decide to try delegating on an experimental basis. It was not much of a relief for him at first, because he felt a hundred hesitations lest his secretary or the service manager would not use as good judgment as he would have used. He secretly looked through their outgoing letters for a few days, just to be sure their decisions would not ruin the business.

"The way this business has grown," he had told the consultants, "has put too many irons in my fire." The irons had been multiplying, true enough, but his policy should have been: Don't touch the irons yourself, delegate the touching to someone else.

He had been touching many of the irons that belonged in the foremen's fires. This made extra work for both the owner and the foremen. The foremen were supervised with the same close attention he had devoted to the morning mail. They were given no leeway in their operations. They had to come to him for decisions on every little point. This made many interruptions for everybody concerned.

It took him four months to make up his mind to put the foremen a little more on their own and keep his hands off their irons.

It was another six months before the foremen began to believe that he meant it, even after they had been given part-time clerks for record-keeping details.

Still more months passed before the foremen overcame their habit of "running to papa" for every decision needed.

It was still longer before they could share some of their responsibilities with the men and women on the production lines. But finally their delegation to the grass roots developed a few utility people who could look after many of the details that two years before had kept the foremen snowed under.

That may seem like slow progress, but it is typical of the snail's pace at which delegating takes hold. It can seldom take place much faster, because of the many adjustments which have to be made in relationships between people, and also in the underlying factors which the executives have to readjust in themselves.

After two years of serious effort to delegate, this was no longer a one-man firm. It became an organization that can nearly run itself, except for the more far-reaching decisions which the owner now has time to anticipate. The firm now has more irons in the fire than before, but because more people have been encouraged and developed to look after the irons, the business operates with much less pressure than when the harassed owner went out to find a psychiatrist.

Among the points this experience highlights is that the need to delegate creeps up and may not be noticed; also that delegating cannot be installed in full bloom, the way the new lighting system can be switched on at once. Delegating gets into operation step-by-step fashion, as habits slowly change and the human climate becomes more permissive for personal initiative.

It usually takes a firm about five years to change from underdelegating to adequate delegating. That five years is for firms which are making a special effort to increase delegating, and where the top executives are behind the change. Some of the larger firms have set up a special vice-president, or a staff department, to spread the gospel and technique of delegating among its executives; it still takes about five years of effort before they begin to feel they are out of the woods. When a situation which needs delegating is left to work itself out, what is most likely to happen is that the woods become thicker [13, 78, 84].

Some other points are highlighted which are worth a separate section. They deal with some blind spots in human nature.

Seeing through some blind spots in delegating

Our owner-manager had heard about delegating but didn't do anything about it until he was caught in a jam. He knew that top executives of big organizations were supposed to delegate, but hadn't thought about its usefulness in small firms or at the grass roots.

By temperament and training he was inclined to think

in terms of tangible objects. An intangible such as delegating was "just so much theory" to him. His first comment was: "The foreman's job is to get out production; show me where there is any production in delegating."

The need for delegating can thus be urgent, but overlooked, or actually denied. Some kinds of people appear to be especially vulnerable in this regard [80, 85].

William B. Given Jr.'s long business experience has led him to conclude that engineers are likely to overlook or dodge delegating. Their training has dealt with tangibles, and they have been taught to do it themselves on their own slide rules. Mr. Given himself is an engineer; he went with the American Brake Shoe Company shortly after graduating from technical college and became president when he was forty-three. He believes in delegating right down to the bottom of the line, in all sixty of their plants [40, 41].

Dr. Myles L. Mace, of the Harvard Graduate School of Business, and a long-time adviser on small business to the U.S. Department of Commerce, has observed that the need for delegating is usually urgent in the small firm that is growing; or where management tries to keep the payrolls down; or, the owner of a small business may hire more help but not delegate, which only adds to his load [72].

Our owner-manager who went looking for a psychiatrist had all those blind spots: a growing small business, payroll pinching, and he was an engineer.

What finally convinced him that delegating might be worth anything it cost was this double-barreled question: "What would happen to production if one of your foremen, as you fear, had to go to a sanitarium and there were no understudies who could handle his job details? And what would happen to the business if you went out of circulation next month?"

His going to the consultants was a form of delegating—he was getting help from experts in reaching some weighty conclusions. He had habitually delegated some of his problems on taxes, advertising, and legal questions to experts. But until the crisis we have described, he had not thought of delegating smaller parts of the job to those doing the smaller jobs.

Thus it is helpful to have some way for spotting where and when the need for delegating arises, and *before underdelegating precipitates a crisis.* We will give two sets of guides which can be used to spot the need for delegating before one gets too far out on the limb. One set can be used by the individual to size up his own status in delegating. The other set can be used by the firm to locate the places up and down the line where more delegating is needed.

Most of these guides are derived from successful executive experience, but some of them have come from recent researches in industrial psychology and sociology. We will call these guides symptoms, because they should be looked upon as indicating some form of managerial disease, which can be called underdelegating.

Personal symptoms of underdelegating

These guides may help some see the need for delegating, despite any blind spots. Each symptom on the guide is usually due to, or leads to, underdelegating.

The guides reflect the many ways in which under-delegating may affect the effectiveness of an individual. They also help spot the personal or policy reasons which may cause some underdelegating.

All in all, they give a quick summary of what delegating is and does.

A "Yes" answer usually points to the need for more delegating, though there are other factors to consider. Unless there is some clear other reason for the "Yes" answer, it should be looked upon as a warning that further analysis and action is called for to increase delegating.

The blank lines following each question provide space for outlining appropriate corrective action to be taken in case of a "Yes" answer. Usually no action is called for when the answer is "No." There is no single "right" answer for these actions. The best action in one situation might not be the best for an executive in a different situation. Each executive has to decide for himself the actions which best fit his present position.

Do you need to delegate more?

1. Do you have to take work home almost every night?   YES   NO
Why? ....
Outline actions you can take to cut this down
....

2. Do you work longer hours than those you supervise or than is usual for hourly-paid workers in the business?   YES   NO
Steps you could take to change this to a "No" answer ....

3. Do you have little time for appointments,
recreation, study, civic work, etc.?   YES   NO
Time could be obtained by ....

....

4. Do you need two or more telephones to keep up
with the job?   YES   NO
How did this happen to come about? ....
Plans for doing something about it ....

....

5. Are you frequently interrupted because others
come to you with questions or for advice or
decisions?   YES   NO
Why does this happen? ....
Strategies for cutting down these interruptions

....

6. Do your employees feel they should not make
work decisions themselves, but should bring all
problems to you?   YES   NO
Examples ....
To change this situation you could ....

....

7. Do you spend some of your working time doing
things for others which they could do for
themselves?   YES   NO
Such as ....
Actions you might take to avoid this ....

....

8. Do you have unfinished jobs accumulating, or
difficulty meeting deadlines?   YES   NO
Examples ....
The jobs could be finished in time by ....

....

9. Do you spend more of your time working on
details than on planning and supervising? YES NO
Why? ....
For a better balance, you could ....

....

10. Do you feel you must keep close tab on the details
if someone is to do a job right? YES NO
Examples ....
Different plans for control of results would be

....

11. Do you work at details because you enjoy them,
although someone else could do them well
enough? YES NO
Such as ....
What to do about this ....

....

12. Are you inclined to keep a finger in everything
that is going on? YES NO
Examples ....
Procedures to try instead ....

....

13. Do you lack confidence in your workers' abilities
so that you are afraid to risk letting them take
over more details? YES NO
Examples ....

....

14. Are you too conscientious (a perfectionist) with
details that are not important for the main
objectives of your position? YES NO
Examples ....
New plans to try for this ....

....

15. Do you keep job details secret from workers, so
    one of them will not be able to displace you?   YES   NO
    Examples ....
    New plans for action ....
    ....

16. Do you believe that an executive should be
    rushed in order to justify his salary?   YES   NO
    Why? ....
    An executive's principal job is ....
    ....

17. Do you hesitate to admit that you need help to
    keep on top of your job?   YES   NO
    Examples of help you could use ....
    List subordinates who could be trained to give
    this help ....
    ....

18. Do you neglect to ask workers for their ideas
    about problems that arise in their work?   YES   NO
    Examples ....
    To change this you could ....
    ....

Company symptoms of underdelegating

Underdelegating is usually a company-wide problem
because of two factors. One factor is found in some policies
and procedures which interfere with the usual processes
of delegating; bureaucratic organizations provide a common example. The other factor is in the human climate
which is usually set by the top layer of executives.

A separate list of guide-questions is needed to uncover
the symptoms when underdelegating has been produced
by policies, procedures, and high-level personnel.

As with the preceding list, each "Yes" answer suggests

that there is underdelegating. And the actions to be taken to correct it will also depend upon each company's situation; the action that corrected the difficulty at the Simplex Company may not be effective in the situation prevailing in the Multiplex Company.

DOES THE ORGANIZATION NEED TO DELEGATE MORE?

1. Do older men predominate in key positions, especially at the middle levels?   YES   NO
   How did this come about? ....
   New policies to consider ....

   ....

2. Is there a shortage of men trained to take over key places in case of deaths or resignations?   YES   NO
   Positions where this is the case ....
   Actions to start regarding this ....

   ....

3. Are key men so tied to their jobs that they lack time to take part in community services and other public-relations activities?   YES   NO
   Which men? ....
   This could be changed by ....

   ....

4. Are some individuals filling two or more key spots?   YES   NO
   Who, and why? ....
   Possible job realignments are ....

   ....

5. Are key men so occupied by current details that they cannot plan future moves, thus causing the firm to move slowly in meeting competition or in changing markets or processes?   YES   NO
   Examples ....

Remedies to consider ....

....

6. Are key men spending part of their time in actual
   production work? YES NO
   Which men? ....
   Their positions could be reorganized by ....

....

7. Are key men kept under such tight control they
   are afraid to delegate? YES NO
   Examples ....
   Other controls which might be used are ....

....

8. Are key men who have been promoted still
   carrying some details from their previous jobs? YES NO
   What men? What details? ....
   Plans for restructuring their positions ....

....

9. Do standard practices, job simplification, rules
   and procedures work against delegating in the
   enterprise? YES NO
   Which practices, etc.? ....
   Alternate arrangements might be ....

....

10. Is the ratio of private secretaries and assistants
    below average? YES NO
    The gains and losses from this are ....
    Areas where this might be changed are ....

....

11. Is decision making (plans, methods, job problems,
    etc.) restricted to a few individuals or specialists? YES NO
    Examples ....
    This could safely be placed on more shoulders by

....

12. Is official criticism for blunders marked enough
to make key people hesitate to use their initiative
or to take risks?   YES   NO
Examples ....
Possible changes worth trying ....
....

13. Are key personnel pitted against each other, so
that they strive to win personal credit rather than
to build a team?   YES   NO
Examples ....
Policy changes this suggests ....
....

14. Is it the practice to promote hard workers, or
"balls of fire," before they have developed
understudies to take their places?   YES   NO
Examples ....
This might be done differently by ....
....

15. Has it been necessary to go outside the firm to
find replacements for key men?   YES   NO
Examples ....
What policy reconsiderations does this suggest?
....

16. Do capable younger employees resign before
their full abilities can be used by the firm?   YES   NO
Examples ....,
This suggests that we should ....
....

17. Do the rank and file of workers seem to lack
initiative?   YES   NO
Possible policy reasons for this ....
Actions that might change it ....
....

18. Do production workers seem to lack job interest, or lack satisfaction with what they do on their jobs?   YES   NO
Examples ....
Delegating might help this by ....
....

19. Does the firm have the reputation of being a one-man company, or has life insurance, payable to the firm, been taken out on some men?   YES   NO
Who? ....
Long-range problems this poses are ....
....

Other factors than underdelegating may, of course, be a cause of some of those symptoms. But underdelegating and nothing else can cause any of them.

Some of the symptoms may merely indicate that a particular key man is basically not qualified for the position he is trying to fill. Delegating, in the form of capable assistants, has been a help in such instances. But such delegating is not a cure-all for the incompetent, although it may enable them to manage more successfully, provided the delegate is not interfered with too much.

On the other hand, it is astonishing, once we look into its ramifications as these guide lists do, to see the ways in which delegating can strengthen both the individual and the enterprise. In the next chapter we will see what bearing this has on executive success.

4

DELEGATING
FOR
EXECUTIVE
SUCCESS

No organization without delegation

The material with which all executives work is man-power. The chief tool for executives to use with this material is delegation. The powers and abilities of individuals are channeled and organized by delegating so that the executive gets things done through others.

Every company of any size draws up an organization chart sooner or later. The chart may have some bearing on salary levels, but its most practical meaning is the way it shows who is responsible for what, and the directions in which an individual executive can delegate his responsibilities and powers. The chart represents the nervous system of the business, showing where impulses for getting

40

things done should be transmitted for the most efficient use of manpower [96].

The chart does not work of itself. There have to be impulses transmitted. Some of the impulses are communications of information or of attitudes. The impulses of most concern to us at present are delegations that are passed along and which stimulate the chart to hum with the activity of shared purposes.

There are numerous firms which have ideal organization charts on paper but have difficulty getting the chart to work out in actual practice. They sometimes change the chart in the hope that a shift or two will put some life into it. Sometimes these shifts produce improvements.

But when an organization does not function as smoothly and profitably as the paper chart indicates it should, the first difficulty to look for is insufficient or incorrect delegating. Active delegations of duties and responsibilities have to keep flowing through the chart to keep it in healthy working condition. When delegated duties stop flowing through some part of the chart, that part has good chances of becoming numb and lifeless; putting a man who knows how to delegate in charge of that section of the chart may bring it back to life.

Donald K. David, the foods executive who became dean of the Harvard Graduate School of Business, told a conference of business leaders: "Delegation and control are the principal functions for the development of the greatest effectiveness of a management team" [13].

In other words, organization is merely a piece of paper without delegating. And delegating without the right kind of control, which we take up in a later chapter, is often the equivalent of neglect of duty.

The extent of spontaneous delegating

How much, and how well, does the average leader delegate?

There is an answer from an analysis of 500 groups which was made by Dr. John K. Hemphill, who is now with the Personnel Research Board at Ohio State University. The task or work groups he studied all had face-to-face leaders. The groups ranged from foundry gangs to bomber crews, from ladies' uplift organizations to office forces of girls [47].

This is a summary of what he found:

Always delegated	25% of the leaders
Frequently delegated	39
Occasionally delegated	15
Seldom delegated	7
Never delegated	2
Did not apply	9
Could not tell	3

We can look upon those figures as showing how much the average person in a position of leadership uses delegation when left to his own devices. Not many of these leaders had studied a book on delegating or were making intentional use of any techniques for delegating. Their delegating was probably spontaneous and not planned, an expression of their individual inclinations, or forced on them to make their jobs more manageable.

With that as a basis, we would conclude that around two-thirds of those who reach some degree of leadership always or frequently make use of delegation.

How effectively they delegate is another question which we will take up in due course. For the time being, we should look upon these leaders' delegating as of the spontaneous, or common garden variety, and not the kind the trained leader or skilled administrator uses.

The small share of these groups to which delegation did not seem to apply could be accounted for mostly by the few social groups that were included in the wide sample of 500 groups.

The successful leaders delegated most

Where delegating did apply, the leader's use of the common garden variety had a significant bearing on his success in leading his group. The followers sized up their 500 leaders as follows:

Good, or excellent leaders	73%
Fair, poor, or bad leaders	27

The good and excellent leaders were found to be the ones who made the most use of delegating.

The failures were concentrated among those who never, seldom, or occasionally delegated.

That difference was great enough to mean that the successful leader was likely to do most delegating in general, even though it was the untrained variety of delegating.

Another comparison shows how near the top delegating ranked as a technique which contributed to leadership success. Dr. Hemphill measured the bearing that seventy different leadership techniques had on the success of the leaders. Delegating came out in the top fourth.

This listing of some of the seventy techniques will give a clear idea of how delegating ranks. Both lists are arranged in order of decreasing significance. The behavior toward the top of the list had most bearing on leadership success.

More significant than delegating:
Making good plans
Making good decisions
Being counted on in the tough spots
Seeing both sides of a question
Making rules and regulations clear
A willing cooperator
Remembering when a follower did a good job

Less significant than delegating:
Showing moral courage
Liking people in general
Easy to talk to
Sticking to his word
Very interested in the group's success
Trying to do a good job
Working harder and longer than others
Knowing technical details of the job
Keeping his group informed about things concerning them
Sticking his neck out for the group
Believing in the group's purpose
Showing physical courage
Putting the job before anything else
Having confidence in one's own decisions
Having plenty of time to spend with the group

Practically no bearing on leadership success:
Being well dressed
Making decisions quickly
Ruling the group firmly
Allowing exceptions to the rules

Many of the techniques in those lists are interwoven into the management objectives, underlying factors in management behavior, and leadership functions we outlined earlier. It may be worth reviewing those to see in which classification each of the techniques would fall.

How effectively do sales executives delegate?

We have found that about two-thirds of the leaders delegated, either always or frequently. But how effective is this spontaneous, untrained delegating? Scattered reports available from ongoing businesses will give us a picture of the quality of delegating. Is it good enough to put real life into the organization charts?

We will start with sales executives. At a session of the National Sales Executives Graduate School, Dr. Charles L. Lapp, of Washington University, gave a report on how thirty-eight companies judged the effectiveness of their sales executives in delegating, and also in other executive methods [61].

First off, the top managements sized up 35 per cent of their sales executives as often failing in delegating.

Additional light on the quality of their delegating came when top management was asked: "What do you feel are the three chief shortcomings of your sales executives?" Here are the ten that topped the list. The items marked * should be looked upon as tied in with delegating; an executive can't delegate effectively, for instance, unless he is also in contact with his workers and has their respect.

*Not enough direct contact with salesmen
Did not keep up with changing trends
Failed to delegate
Not enough original ideas
*Too little time spent in planning
*Inability to obtain subordinates' respect
*Too much time spent on routine details
Unwilling to study and prepare for the job
Failed to obtain cooperation of other executives
Inability to make quick and sound decisions

Notice that those functions do not work out exactly the same with sales managers as with the 500 more general leaders. Inability to make quick decisions counted for little among the more general leaders, but top management regarded it as important among sales executives. This probably reflects a tendency for various specialized positions to have special requirements which may not apply to some other executive positions.

Perhaps a predominant reason for the poor showing of these sales managers in delegating is that they would rather be out selling than in executive positions where they had to keep the selling section of the organization chart running smoothly.

Executives who weren't making good

"Why did one particular executive in your company fail?" Dr. Frederick J. Gaudet, of the Laboratory of Psychological Studies at Stevens Institute of Technology, asked 200 firms. Three reasons were given most frequently, and each applied to about 10 per cent of the failing executives [38]:

Not delegating responsibility
Lack of breadth of knowledge
Failure to analyze and evaluate

Of lesser importance, and in decreasing order as listed, were:

Poor in judging people
Not cooperating with others
Weakness in making decisions
Weakness in knowledge of organization and administration

The situation in one firm

The excellent and the below-average executives of one business supply corporation have also been compared in their use of delegation. This comparison was made by Dr. Earl Brooks, of the New York State School of Industrial and Labor Relations, at Cornell University [7].

He checked the top 96 executives. They were rated on a large assortment of characteristics and work methods, not only by their immediate superiors but also by their own employees. About the same number of executives were judged excellent as were judged below average. The superiors' reports averaged out thus:

	DELEGATED EFFECTIVELY
Excellent executives	73%
Below-average executives	zero

There was obviously not much chance for an executive to be considered excellent unless he delegated effectively.

Dr. Brooks also analyzed other records of the executives' methods. The following gives a quick rundown, the items toward the top of the list having most bearing on executive success in this corporation. It is worth keeping in mind that most of the items on the list are usually involved in effective delegating. For instance, we have to select the right person to delegate to, have workers take part in some decision making, and so on through the list, to make delegating work and the organization chart work.

They almost always, or always:	EXCELLENT EXECUTIVES	BELOW-AVERAGE EXECUTIVES
Had workers share in making decisions	100%	10%
Coordinated the activities of workers	100	10
Made full use of skills and abilities of workers	100	10
Let workers know how they were doing	83	zero
Saw that authority of each worker was clearly understood	83	10
Kept workers informed of activities in other departments	83	10
Kept workers informed about things affecting their work	92	20
Encouraged workers to exchange information	92	20
Knew how well workers were doing	100	30
Encouraged workers to express their ideas and opinions	100	30
Selected the right person for the job	100	30

Such records indicate strongly that delegating counts in executive success. We could sum the records up by saying that delegating ranks in the top quarter of methods used by executives. Obviously, the individual executive is wise to acquire skill in delegating, so that he can use something better than the common garden variety.

Many managements are alert to the importance of delegating skills, and use various methods of sizing up their executives in this regard. In the next chapter we will see some of the ways this is done.

Modern emphasis on delegating

Sometimes a man acts like an unloved wife as he asks: "How *does* one get ahead in this firm?"

Many skills are needed to get ahead. But in every survey which has included delegating, it has come out among the top 25 per cent of skills that make for executive success.

In case you are now in supervisory work, the odds are high that your chief has been instructed to size up the way you delegate. He does this sizing up informally but continually. He keeps an eye on other points, of course, because delegating is only one of the methods in the top fourth.

Perhaps your chief has never mentioned directly to you what he thinks about your delegating skills, either to find fault or to give a pat on the back. Perhaps he hasn't given you much help or coaching to improve in delegating. But he should mention it, and he should coach you [37].

In many firms salaried employees are rated once or twice a year on the effectiveness of their delegating. When this is done, the ratings are usually talked over with the man rated. His chief tries to explain why the rating is high or why it is not as high as it might have been. And he also gives suggestions about how to perform so the rating is higher for the next period.

These ratings are almost always a crucial factor when time comes to decide who gets a promotion. It sometimes happens that a long-service man who is rated low in delegating finds himself left behind by the promotion-review committee.

This emphasis on delegating, rather new, is understandable. Operational details multiply as firms grow. The details also increase because of competition, the complications of new materials and processes, and tax, labor, and legal demands. One man may not have enough eyes and arms—and time—to take care of the administrative details of a single department. He has to delegate the responsibilities assigned him on the organization chart in order to operate effectively.

Small business is in the same boat. A firm can be small in numbers employed but still have about the same details to look after as its giant competitors. We will see shortly how this has almost trapped some members of the Young Presidents' Organization, young executives who are running small or medium-sized businesses [72].

It is usually the larger or more progressive firm which does the most about delegating. Since World War II there has been a rapid increase in the number of firms which have set up departments for management development or for executive training. Delegating is one of the skills these departments hammer away at, whether with a young trainee on his first job or a long-time employee the firm is trying to upgrade [23].

Most of these development programs include periodic checks on the individual's progress. His current working methods are judged against the objectives the training is aimed to achieve. These periodic performance reviews pin-point (a) the skills in which the person is ready for a higher job, and (b) those in which he needs to improve before being promoted. All these reviews include skill in delegating, in one guise or another.

Only a little reflection is needed to understand why delegating skill often tips the balance in promotions. Each step up the ladder adds to the scope of duties for which the executive is responsible. It is seldom humanly possible to do them all singlehandedly. He has to delegate to avoid being snowed under with details which can keep him off the main track of his job objectives. He also has to delegate to train understudies who can keep things humming in his absence.

Here are some arbitrary figures which are used to illustrate the need for more delegating with each step up the ladder:

POSITION	HOW MANY OF ITS FUNCTIONS SHOULD BE DELEGATED
President	95%
Vice-president	75
Department head	50
Foreman	25

Those percentages are off-the-cuff estimates, and leeway has to be allowed. But the figures show the need for delegating skill as a personal aid for getting ahead. The figures also remind us that the higher one goes, the more one is dependent upon getting things done through others, if the organization chart is to produce results. The man who is himself a worldbeater for working, may or may not be worth his beans in getting work done through others by delegating.

The person who wants to get ahead in a modern organization needs to do some soul searching about just where he stacks up in delegating skill. There are not many "natural born delegators." Usually the skill is picked up, sometimes intentionally, sometimes accidentally. Picking it up intentionally is one aim of training programs.

The usual first step toward picking it up intentionally is to find out how one already stands in delegating skill, and what his weak points may be in delegating. That is where rating scales are useful, although sometimes the ratings are embarrassing. The help can be permanent, and the embarrassment only temporary.

How rating scales help

Skill in delegating cannot yet be measured as accurately as typing skill or as one's general intelligence. The ratings for delegating skill probably give only a rough approximation.

Their usefulness does not depend as much upon great accuracy, however, as upon the effect they have in making people more delegating-minded. This effect is produced both in the person rated and in the person making the rating. It is considered wholesome for both of them.

One large chemical firm is satisfied with the simple report that the man's skill in delegating is a strong factor, or a hindering factor, in his qualifications for the next job ahead of him. It does not make a pretense of being accurate to an exact per cent.

When delegating skill is judged to be a hindering factor, the superior talks it over with the man. Together they work out plans for improvement. These plans include not only some intentional self-development, but usually also some practical experience in delegating which the superior devises for him.

The practical-experience route gives the man an opportunity to learn delegating by actually delegating. It gives him actual practice to fill the gaps, and perhaps correct some errors, in his theoretical thinking about it. It is difficult to find any training combination that is better than actual experience combined with good coaching.

It is often noted that most people who have been given supervisory work have had no previous experience in delegating. This may account for most of them underdelegating. And it also makes it difficult to judge in advance how well the man might delegate if he were promoted.

By providing opportunities for practice in delegating, these dual handicaps are cut down. The chief himself has to use some delegation to provide opportunities for those under him to practice delegating. Vocational counselors often advise capable young men to give preference to the job where the chief has a reputation for delegating; that job will most likely give the newcomer the kind of experiences that will do most to develop his executive potentials.

The Westinghouse appraisal

The Westinghouse Electric Corporation rates on the following broad aspects in managerial development:

1. What he is
2. What he knows
3. How he works
4. What he accomplishes

Each of these four is broken down into smaller elements on which the man is rated. He is rated, not in percentages, but as: Outstanding, Very high, Satisfactory, Below satisfactory, or Unsatisfactory.

Delegating has considerable bearing on "What he accomplishes," but for the purposes of appraisal it is included in the "How he works" category:

__ Planning
__ Organizing
__ Communicating
__ Following through
__ Developing people
__ Maintaining morale
__ Working with others
__ Delegating

Although delegating is rated separately, the person's skill in delegating will also have some influence upon his ratings on Communicating, Developing people, and Maintaining morale [107].

The U.S. Rubber rating

The tire division of the United States Rubber Company acts on the policy that "the future of the company is largely dependent upon, among other things, its ability to develop personnel capable of performing effectively on assignments of managerial responsibility" [104].

The men in its management development program are rated on six broad aspects of the skills and methods which are considered necessary in managerial work:

Acceptability
Analyzing
Leadership
Making decisions
Organizing ability (Delegating)
Responsibility

Organizing ability (Delegating) is given separate treatment because: A man's "success and an evidence of his organizing ability depend not so much on his own work output as upon his ability to arrange for such work output by the development of an effective team of competent people who thoroughly understand and are able to discharge the obligations of their respective positions," and "the organized executive is usually freed from the necessity of handling a heavy load of details—the rightful share of which others could and should be trained to assume—a load which limits and restricts the dimensions of his own usefulness."

This form is used in rating the man's skill in delegating to organize his work and employees:

ORGANIZING ABILITY—*Ability to arrange for the accomplishment of his job responsibility in an orderly, efficient manner.*

Review in your mind the individual's performance in relation to the following questions:

Has he divided his work into the different tasks which make up his total job responsibility? Does he concentrate on one or two parts of his responsibility so that little is accomplished on the rest of his job? Does he show that he is willing to delegate responsibility and authority? Does he give responsibility to others but fail to give them authority to carry it out? Does he feel that if the job is to be done right he must do it himself? Does he control the activity without destroying the initiative of those who are working for him?

Now check one of the following that most accurately describes the individual:

___ Poorly organized. Tries to do everything himself.

___ Little organized approach by delegation. Overburdens self with details.

___ Some attempt at delegation on normal, routine affairs. Needs guidance on major changes.

___ Successful in apportioning work load effectively. Needs little guidance in co-ordinating major efforts.

___ Delegates authority very effectively. Recognizes broad objectives clearly and arranges for most effective accomplishment.

At McKesson & Robbins, Inc.

All 900 McKesson & Robbins executives are included in the management-development program. Chairman George van Gorder told these men that this was done because they wanted to accomplish two purposes:

"First, to make our present first team of management men stronger, to make it function smoothly, and to make it more efficient.

"Second, to develop qualified reserves. Just as we have reserves for building and equipment and for future expansion, so we must have reserves of men trained ready to step into more responsible positions.

"We know of no program that we have ever launched that is more vital than this one. Our first job must be the building of men who can manage other men with understanding and confidence."

This program has been carried out by seminar discussions, sound slides, special readings, and by ratings. The once-a-year ratings answer the question "How am I doing?" The discussions and readings help answer "How can I improve?" Both these phases are given about equal emphasis [70].

Ratings are made on four general aspects:

Executive abilities
Job performance
Knowledge, training, and experience
Personal qualities

Skill in delegating is included, both directly and indirectly, in the ratings on Executive abilities. A study of the company's rating form for this can help us discover some of the elements which also bear indirectly on delegating. Delegating does not stand alone in actual practice, but in relationship to other executive skills or methods or techniques—a common thread appearing in many procedures used by executives in getting things done through others.

Below is the rating form used with the McKesson & Robbins executives.

It is possible to construct a rating scale for delegating skills which would be much more detailed than the examples given. It could include most of the techniques which are used in delegating, and to which the balance of this book is devoted. Some readers might find that trying to draw up such a detailed rating scale, after reading through

```
┌─────────────────── 2.  EXECUTIVE ABILITIES ───────────────────┐
│         Ability to Plan and Organize Work            RATING    │
│         Needs                    Needs               SCALE     │
│      OK Help                  OK Help                          │
│      ☐  ☐  Plans his own work well  ☐  ☐  Organizes the work of │
│                                            others well   Out-  │
│      ☐  ☐  Plans the work of others ☐  ☐  Follows up standing  │
│             well                           effectively         │
│      ☐  ☐  Organizes his own work well                         │
│      COMMENT: _____       Excel-    │
│                                                      lent      │
│         Ability to Select and Develop Personnel                │
│         Needs                    Needs                          │
│      OK Help                  OK Help                          │
│      ☐  ☐  Selects new employees   ☐  ☐  Delegates responsibili-│
│             well                          ties properly  Good  │
│      ☐  ☐  Trains new employees    ☐  ☐  Recognizes promotable  │
│             well                          employees            │
│      ☐  ☐  Explains new work well  ☐  ☐  Builds morale effectively│
│      COMMENT: _____        Fair     │
│            Ability to Make Decisions                           │
│         Needs                                                   │
│      OK Help                                         Poor      │
│      ☐  ☐  Makes decisions willingly                           │
│      ☐  ☐  Makes minor decisions well                          │
│      ☐  ☐  Makes major decisions well               ☐         │
│      COMMENT: _____      No Rating  │
└────────────────────────────────────────────────────────────────┘
```

the book, would give them a more certain grasp of delegating's ins and outs. Although the rating scale would probably be too long for general usefulness, it would doubtless be valuable for some individuals.

Is too much delegating possible?

Surveys show that the weakness, with both individuals and firms, is most likely to be underdelegating. No firm we know of has yet rated its executives on overdelegating.

But note should be made that overdelegation sometimes does occur [92].

It is difficult to tell where overdelegation leaves off and neglect begins. This was the case with a man in his middle thirties who had built up a profitable one-man insurance agency. His office girl was capable, and he delegated more and more to her and didn't know where to stop. Soon he was spending most of his time playing golf or pinochle, or fishing, leaving the girl to run the business.

People who like to take things easy, as that insurance man did, are susceptible to delegating too much. Those who like to show their importance also may surround themselves with assistants who are not needed and to whom they delegate too much.

Delegating too soon is a close relative of delegating too much. Too soon means before the person delegated to is capable of carrying on without supervision. This happened recently on a large scale with a manufacturer of heavy machinery.

In a splurge of expansion, this firm made bargain purchases of several small companies. Men from the parent firm were delegated to operate the new divisions. Most of these men, however, had not been adequately groomed for their heavier responsibilities; too much was delegated to them too soon.

In addition, the central office did not keep in close enough touch with the remote operations. The divisions were sapping the financial resources of the parent corporation because of this lack of control.

This firm's predicament reminds us that we cannot safely delegate and forget. We must delegate, but watch and lend a helping hand as soon as the help is needed. Control and freedom have to be properly balanced: more control while the man is developing, more freedom after the rating scales show he can be trusted with it.

The pitfall of overdelegating without keeping adequate control was illustrated by two U.S. Presidents, Grant and

Harding. Each delegated right and left, without much attention to the capabilities or intentions of the people delegated to. Neither of these presidents kept any control on most of the operations delegated. As an over-all result, historians rate Grant and Harding as the two failures among our Presidents [1].

The possibility of overdelegating, or abdicating, is one of the reasons why cut-and-dried rules cannot be followed. Adequate delegating remains an art. It is not picked up from a book read on some week end.

Practice, through stages of progressively more and more delegating, is usually essential to get one into the swing. The "school of hard knocks" remains a good teacher—for pupils who will learn from it.

Dr. John H. Gorsuch, of the U.S. Steel Corporation, has observed that "time, effort, and persistence are needed to develop the art." It is usually conceded that several years of effort are needed, even under favorable conditions [43].

This helps explain the plight of the members of the Young Presidents' Organization. This group consists mostly of self-made young men who have risen rapidly by their skill and dispatch in doing things themselves. They have not been "seasoned" by the usual course of hard knocks. But as presidents they have to depend more upon getting things done through others—something in which they have not, as a rule, had much practice. Consequently, they have to remodel many of their working methods.

Lyle M. Spencer, of Science Research Associates, himself a young president, has surveyed other young presidents. He reports: "Learning to delegate authority—really doing it rather than just paying lip service—is one of the most complicated skills a new president must master when he takes his seat in the front office" [94, 95].

Picking up the art is also complicated by sociological factors which are too often overlooked. The organization chart is usually based on pure logic, showing how responsibilities and delegations might be channeled under ideal conditions. If conditions were ideal, there would not be much need for art in delegating. But there are always sociological factors in any organization which keep conditions from being logical and ideal. We turn to some of these in the following chapter.

6

SOCIOLOGICAL ASPECTS OF DELEGATING

1. Social sensitivity helps delegating

2. Size, cohesiveness, and uniformity of groups

3. Group rigidity, selectivity, and goals

4. Turnover, intimacy, and independence

5. Control, fulfillingness, and pleasantness

Social sensitivity helps delegating

It is difficult to delegate successfully to one worker without considering his relationships to other workers. This is because we live and work in webs of interrelations with various groups of people. These webs are the special province of the rising science of industrial sociology. These webs may seem illogical, or even foolish, but they exert a tremendous power over people [5, 15, 17, 50, 56, 79].

During a rush period, for instance, one department manager delegated his spinster secretary to follow through on some inspection details with a crew of machinists who were in government production. The crew's output and morale went down almost at once. The men claimed that their output went down due to the closer inspections and rejects which cut into their piece-rate earnings.

Then one of the machinists quit his job. The manager had a long talk with him. Several things the man said prompted the manager to suspect that the real cause of the unrest in that crew was that he had delegated the inspection detail to a woman. She had been capable, and fair in handling the responsibility, but had caught the manager in a web.

The machinists had chafed when other crews teased them about working for a woman boss. The machinists had always been proud of doing a real man's work, but now they felt they were being sissified.

Acting on this diagnosis of the sociological aspects, the manager shifted the inspection detail to one of the machinists. He had avoided this when he delegated to his secretary, because there was a shortage of skilled operators. But the first week of delegation to the machinist saw an increase in production, although the man delegated to was out of direct production about a fourth of his time.

None of the machinists ever mentioned the "sissifying episode" to the manager, but apparently they sensed why he made the change and were grateful for the way he had helped them save face. Several months later, when he was in real trouble with another group of workers, this group of machinists came to his side and shifted the tide in his favor.

Delegating has to be planned to fit the notions of what that particular group thinks is "fit and proper." The person delegated to has to work with, or through, or in cooperation with, other workers. He may talk to only one person at a time, but that one person remains a member of his work group and is often more influenced by what that group thinks than by the person who is trying to carry out the delegation.

Groups have their own "personalities" which are as distinctive as those of individuals. Work crews, yard gangs, office staffs, even research teams have their own group peculiarities and loyalties. Some groups respond to their leaders' gentle suggestions, while with other groups the whip has to be cracked. The techniques that make for successful leadership with the office force of young business school graduates may not work in the prison tailor shop [18].

Characteristics which are outstanding in the "personalities" of groups have been analyzed by Dr. John K. Hemphill, whom we first met in Chapter 4. He found that different group "personalities" posed different problems for the leaders—one reason there are exceptions to all rules, and why delegating is, to a large degree, an art [47, 48].

He found some kinds of groups where delegating meant much more for leadership success than in other kinds of groups—reminding us, again, to size up the group and plan the delegating accordingly.

To help in sizing up group "personalities," we will give thumbnail descriptions of the way groups, or work teams, show their "personalities." These descriptions are the ones used by Dr. Hemphill in his breakdowns.

Familiarity with these group characteristics should sharpen one's social sensitivity—the awareness of social pressures and the directions in which they are pushing typical members of the groups; such as that crew of machinists who balked when they felt they were being treated as sissies. (You may want to refresh your concepts on social sensitivity by looking back into section 6 of Chapter 2.)

There is a good chance that delegating, and leadership in general, will fizzle unless the leader is a good judge of the pressures that are operating within the group. This may seem like the tail wagging the dog, but such is often the case.

Size, cohesiveness, and uniformity of groups

Differences in *size of group* is a good one to begin with, if for no other reason than that it is easily observed. Size may seem to be a superficial aspect, but it does make a considerable difference. Dr. Hemphill found that the suc-

Groups composed of three persons have a tendency to break up into a twosome, with one member left outside as an isolate.

cessful leader of a large group (more than thirty people) is more likely to have to be firm and impersonal in his relations with the members. The corporal over four men may be lax, and show favoritism, but not the captain of the larger company.

The leader of the larger group is also likely to have more job pressure on him, which may force him to delegate, whether he is in favor of the idea or not.

An interesting observation of the significance of size of the group has been reported by Dr. Mason Haire, University of California psychologist. In a large utility company about one hundred girls sorted bills in a large room. Their output was below expectations, absenteeism high, and morale in general was low.

Then some structural changes were made in the building. While these changes were under way it was necessary for the girls to be broken up into small groups of about ten girls in each group. An efficiency engineer might not have approved of this change because it caused extra walking for supplies and made supervision more difficult. Yet there was a great improvement in output, morale, and job attendance that was due solely to the groups being smaller. This gain will be more understandable as we become acquainted with some other sociological aspects of the work situation [45].

The *cohesiveness,* or "feeling of togetherness" which members have, also varies from group to group. There are closely knit office forces and loosely knit ones. Some include the boss in their togetherness, others exclude him. This also varies in families: some have a strong "family feeling"; in others it is every member for himself [17].

Cohesiveness is not as tangible a characteristic as size. But it is important, as any executive knows who has struggled to build a feeling of "one big family" among his employees.

If he delegates mostly to a "crown prince," not much progress should be expected toward building one big family. Those who do not receive any delegations often hold together more cohesively than before, but they form a family of their own, so to speak, rather than a company family. They subtly exert resistance against the crown prince's efforts to get things done through them.

Cohesiveness is also increased when the group feels it is harshly treated, discriminated against, or too-closely supervised. But under these circumstances the cohesiveness results in the group going its own way rather than joining the one big family. This is why many of the early efforts to "break the union" resulted in greater union strength.

Uniformity of membership is another significant characteristic in which groups differ from each other. New office workers just out of parochial business school, for instance, are much like peas from the same pod—about the same age, education, religion, and inexperience. At the other end of the range in uniformity are the mixtures of unlikes, such as the local grievance board which is composed of old and young, religious and irreligious, skilled and unskilled, the ins and the outs, some native Americans, some foreign born.

As a guess, would the pressures within the group make it easier to lead the business college students, or the grievance board? And with which group would more forethought be needed when deciding which member to delegate to?

Group rigidity, selectivity, and goals

Groups vary in the *rigidity* of the way they follow their customary procedures, duties, or details. Bureaucratic groups think in terms of following the book of rules closely. They are likely to be rigid groups, and to resist changes in their usual procedures or ways.

But the sales force in the automobile agency is usually a flexible, or non-rigid, group. Its concern with any rules is principally to ignore or evade them.

Delegating often runs into a stone wall of group pressure when the group's customs are rigidly structured, unless the delegating has been specifically prescribed in the book of procedures. Many business executives have run head on into this wall of pressure when they took a temporary government assignment.

Ritualistic groups, such as lodges, are characterized by rigidity. The "Loyal Worshipful Leader" who comes into office with the idea of "pepping up the ritual" should not expect the committees he delegates to to follow through as he thinks they should.

Large and far-flung corporations may get into similar rigid conditions, unless the central office has patiently trained the branches to be largely self-sufficient, and to accept and pass along delegations. Successful decentralization takes continuous effort from the home office to see that there is not too much, nor too little, rigidity.

There may be some basis for believing that groups of older workers are more likely to have group rigidity than do younger workers.

Groups differ in *selectivity*, or the extent to which they build walls around themselves. Selectivity is as noticeable in work groups as in the old guard of local society.

The requirement of a certain degree of skill, or of a union card, are common examples of selectivity at work in business groups. There are also less obvious selective factors which emerge from the group itself. An example is the initiations and cold shoulder many work groups give to newcomers before accepting them as "our kind of people." About one out of three workers feels that he is not accepted by the others in his work group. This one-out-of-three is an isolate. Absenteeism, turnover, and low production have been found associated with the feeling of being an isolate.

The problems of desegregation hinge largely on group differences in selectivity. White groups in the South are more selective on color than comparable groups in the North.

When a group shows some kind of selectivity, the leader needs astute social sensitivity in order to decide whom to delegate to. An example is the pressure many work groups exert against the expert who has been brought in from outside to handle some powers delegated to him. If the outside expert throws his weight around, he will likely increase their selectivity and also their cohesiveness—all against the objectives for which he is working.

Staff members are also in the position of being looked upon as outsiders in case they have to work with production groups [92].

Some groups have *clear-cut goals,* such as to sandbag

the river bank before the rising water overflows, or to sell more automobiles than a competitor does during the next month.

Clear-cut goals help structure group behavior and attitudes, giving the members a shared objective to work for. This is especially true when the group itself had some part

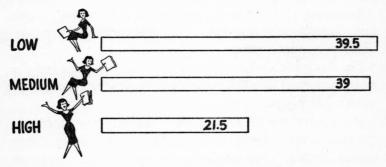

LOW	39.5
MEDIUM	39
HIGH	21.5

Not many work groups have high productivity as a goal. This chart shows the situation in some clerical departments of a large financial institution. Only 21.5 per cent of the workers surveyed had high pride in productivity [81].

in deciding what the goals are to be. This is one reason for the increasing practice of having workers take more part in reaching decisions about their work goals [60].

We will see later that quotas, although they may be specific, should not usually be considered as group goals.

Experience has indicated that delegating is most effective when the objectives are clear-cut and meaningful, and also when they offer a bit of a challenge which the group accepts as worth working for. The sandbagging objective meets those requirements. "Clip these pieces together as they come along the line" does not.

Turnover, intimacy, and independence

The "personality" of groups is also affected by the rate of *turnover of membership.* The sandbagging crew is temporary. The group clipping the two pieces together may be a bit longer lived. The skilled tool makers are a more permanent group—as long as they are not treated as sissies.

In seasonal industries the majority of workers are temporary. Telephone employees, at the other extreme, are relatively permanent groups.

Dr. Hemphill's records showed that delegating played a more important role in leadership success when the groups were relatively permanent.

It is also worth noting that high-member-turnover groups are often fuzzy, or borderline, on the other group characteristics. They often have not existed long enough as groups to form much cohesiveness, or to become rigid in their expectations, or to become selective in whom they look upon as "our kind of people" [17].

A group is something more than a number of people in the same department or at a street corner waiting for the traffic light to change. After a number of people have been together in some common activity for some time, they begin to show signs of group behavior, of having some objectives which they share with each other. They then show some of the dozen or more characteristics of a group "personality." As soon as such characteristics are shown, it is no longer four individuals working in the shipping room, for instance, but a group of four and some group forces, or pressures, will have developed. These pressures make the leadership situation vastly different.

The *intimacy between members* also modifies the "personality" of a group. The intimacy is usually low when the leader has used rivalry to arouse competition between employees. Contests may also lower it.

It is also usually low when the work is paced by an assembly line where workers have little chance to leave their stations or to talk with other workers. Work in noisy locations is also likely to lower the intimacy [105].

In a job shop, on the other hand, the intimacy is usually higher, and often includes the sharing of personal problems with each other. The workers may also informally delegate parts of their jobs to each other, without the boss knowing about the leeway they have taken.

Intimacy is marked, of course, when workers form a clique.

Differences in the degree of intimacy may produce subgroups within a larger work group. This was observed in a large department store by Dr. George F. F. Lombard, professor of human relations at the Harvard Graduate School of Business. The salesgirls for infants' wear showed no intimacy with each other. But at the adjoining counter, the clerks for women's sportswear were markedly intimate, even exchanging tips on how to care for sore feet. The same department manager had to supervise both subgroups [67].

The degree of *independence from other* groups is another variable—whether the group is mostly on its own, or part of a larger organization. The salesclerks in a chain store are part of a larger corporation, which makes their sociological situation different from that which prevails in the independent store. Job details and pay may be the same, but the social forces operating on the groups will not be the same.

Dr. Hemphill found that delegating counted more toward successful leadership when the group is low in independence—that is, when it is a unit in a larger organization. This is reflected in business practice. The larger firms are the ones doing most to have their executives delegate, and to appraise the executive's skill in delegating before he is promoted.

Control, fulfillingness, and pleasantness

Control of personal behavior by the group is another significant variable. In monasteries, and in many professions, this control is marked. Physicians are occasionally dismissed from the medical society purely because of personal conduct.

Some companies try to control personal conduct. There are a few that will not employ a person who uses tobacco. Some banks require that employees ask permission to marry. One large firm prescribes detachable white collars for its white-collar employees. These controls are imposed from above, and do not spring from the group itself.

In most work groups, the group itself does not bother about the personal behavior of its members—they can be vegetarians, nonsmokers, alcoholics, or bigamists for all the group cares.

This poses problems if a leader feels he should exercise some control over his workers' personal conduct. The group will hesitate to back the leader up, and will seldom cooperate with whoever is delegated to carry through a program that aims to change the conduct of group members. A few firms have employed social workers to "improve" employees' personal conduct and home life; the employees have usually given a frigid shoulder to these efforts.

Another example is in suggestions about political candidates who merit the workers' votes. Suggestions from the employer are usually not followed. But suggestions from within the group, as by the union officers, are more often followed.

The *fulfillingness*, or lack of frustration, refers to how well the purpose and activities of the group help the people in it to do what they deeply want to do.

Workers who are drafted into the shop find the job less fulfilling than do those who have chosen shop work because they "get a kick out of it." The work group is probably not as fulfilling as it should be for the person who joined it for the pay or fringe benefits, rather than for the nature of the work itself. Not all draftees are in the military services.

Carefully planned delegating can make a job more fulfilling, at least to the workers delegated to—not, however, if engineering details are delegated to the person who would get more kick, more fulfillment, from looking after clerical details [59, Chap. 9].

Surveys indicate that at least one-fourth of workers have low satisfaction, or actual dissatisfaction, from what they have to do on their jobs. The dissatisfaction (lack of fulfillingness) tends to increase as a job is simplified and there is less variety in things to do. Suitable delegating can put more variety into the job, enlarge it, and make it more fulfilling [81, 105].

Job interest is related to this variable. When workers lack job interest, delegating can often give a real interest. Whenever the problem is to motivate a work group, delegating should be looked into as a way to provide a natural incentive [59, Chap. 12].

The opportunity to use one's initiative and to have some personal responsibility is also related to fulfillingness. Recent research has indicated that this aspect of group forces may have much wider ramifications than might be anticipated. Dr. Robert C. Williamson, of Los Angeles City College, investigated the married happiness of 210 couples and determined the influence of various socioeconomic factors on this happiness. Job satisfaction proved to be desirable, not only for the married happiness of the husband but also for the wife [109].

The *pleasantness* of being in a particular group is another aspect of group "personality." People have been known to change jobs or church affiliations, in order to be with a different group which affords them more pleasure, though the activities and purposes of the old and the new groups are much the same.

Alcoholics who are trying to reform, for example, often find it more pleasurable to "take the cure" in Alcoholics Anonymous than in the WCTU.

When the pleasurableness of being in a particular group is low, Dr. Hemphill found that delegating does not add anything to leadership success. To state it loosely, with emphasis on the other end, delegating is likely to work best when workers are a happy lot. But there is also a circular effect at work, because delegating to the rank and file usually does more than most fringe benefits to make them a happy lot. This illustrates the way delegating often gains momentum, or feeds on itself, by changing relationships so that they become more favorable for effective delegating.

These twelve differences in the "personalities" of groups produce crosscurrents which pull people one way or the other. The currents have washed out many leadership plans which appeared logical on paper, but did not take the crosscurrent, say, of "sissiness," into account.

These group differences, with the exception of size, deal mostly with intangible qualities. The person who is not looking carefully for the differences, or who does not know what differences to look for, may miss them and mumble something about the perversity of human nature when group pressures ruin his plans.

Some deliberate experience in looking for such differences makes them more tangible to the onlooker. Trained sociologists, for instance, can make a fairly accurate estimation of the characteristics of a group after observing it for a short time, or even by conversations about the group with some of its members. Most colleges giving graduate courses in sociology include some special courses for such training.

The modern executive can usually profit if he sharpens his social sensitivity to group pressures. Some of these intangible forces are the most real factors with which he has to operate. These pressures will be less likely to pick his pocket if he can spot them a block away. There will be many examples of them in the balance of the book, and we hope they will serve to increase this sensitivity.

7

**GETTING
READY
TO
DELEGATE**

Attitude as essential as procedures

Frederic H. was proud as a peacock of the work his department turned out, but he didn't like the way he was always kept on the jump. He finally concluded he should reorganize things so that he could delegate.

After that decision he spent several week ends at the office, alone, working like a tornado, as he mapped a reorganization. He had heard General Electric's reorganization praised, so he tried to follow their chart as closely as his little business permitted.

His plan completed, he leaned back and admired the chart he had drawn. "The force will be impressed," he thought to himself, "when I spring this on them and they see how good a draftsman the old boy is."

"Yes sir," he mused half-aloud. "Starting Monday the old boy will be delegating—the conductor of an orchestra."

The departmental meeting had not been under way long on Monday morning when he sensed that he was walking on eggs. No one seemed to understand his plan. They didn't openly find fault. They just asked questions which showed they didn't catch on, and which he had difficulty answering. He got that feeling in his stomach again, which he thought might be due to an ulcer.

He is now sure that delegating is an impractical theory. His own stab at it, however, shows two things about him. For one, he did not have a clear idea of delegating and how to go about it. For the other, he was not ready to delegate, regardless of how keenly he wanted to ease his job burden. If he had been ready to delegate, he would not have drawn up his reorganization plan unaided and as a surprise—or was it a shock?—for his employees; he would have had some of them help him plan it.

Delegating is as much a state of mind as it is a change in the chart, or a plan of assigning duties. Until one has this state of mind, one is not yet ready to delegate successfully.

The leader almost always has to adjust some of his attitudes in order to get in a frame of mind to delegate. Also, he usually has to bide his time patiently until his readiness is reflected in the changed attitudes of his subordinates. Frederic H.'s employees couldn't catch on to his plan largely for this reason.

The attitudes and expectations which make delegating work are developed slowly. One can seldom resolve to delegate more, and then do it effectively from a cold start [89].

There are some people who are so strongly authoritarian in their make-ups that it is almost impossible for them to develop a readiness for real delegating. They can plan subordinates' work and pass out job assignments, but they can't bring themselves to give the freedom for action that delegating demands. As a result, their subordinates can't actually act for them, and there is little gained.

This chapter is devoted to five basic attitudes which the leader needs to have to be ready to start delegating [9, 10, 19].

The office that had double-daylight time

Spur-of-the-moment delegating is seldom effective. This is partly because it has not been thoughtfully planned. But a stronger reason is usually that the attitudes which trigger the impulse are not the sort that make delegating work; there is no readiness worth mentioning, just an intense wish to delegate. This is illustrated by an entertaining mix-up in a small office.

Executives are a fortunate lot. For, as everybody knows, an executive has nothing to do.
That is, except . . .

To decide what is to be done;
To tell somebody to do it;
To listen to reasons why it should not be done;
Why it should be done by somebody else, or why it should be done a different way;
And to prepare arguments in rebuttal that are convincing and conclusive;

To follow up to see if the thing has been done;
To discover that it has not been done;
To inquire why it has not been done;
To listen to excuses from the person who should have done it
and did not do it;
And to think up arguments to overcome the excuses . . .

To follow up a second time to see if the thing has been done;
To discover that it was done, but done incorrectly;
To point out how it should have been done;
To conclude that as long as it has been done it might as well be
left the way it is;

To wonder if it isn't time to get rid of a person who never does
anything correctly;
To reflect that the person at fault has a wife and even children;
And that certainly no other executive in the world would put
up with him for a moment,
And that in all probability any successor would be just as bad,
or worse . . .

To consider how much simpler and better the thing would
have been done had he done it himself in the first place;
To reflect sadly that if he had done it himself he would have
been able to do it right in twenty minutes;
Whereas, as it turned out, it took someone else three weeks to
do it incorrectly;

But, to realize that had he done it himself,
It would have had a very demoralizing effect on the whole organization,
Because it would strike at the very fundamental belief of all
employees

That an executive has nothing to do!

Who wrote this? Let us know if you know.

The last Friday in April one clerk worked a few minutes after the others had left. As she was leaving, she remembered that daylight time began on Sunday. She thoughtfully moved the wall clock ahead one hour.

The boss came in on Sunday afternoon, to catch up on his work—a possible sign that he was already behind the eight ball on delegating. As he was leaving, he remembered daylight time, so he moved the clock ahead another hour.

Monday morning the girls giggled about their extra dose of daylight time, but the boss was in no mood to laugh it off.

"Who monkeyed with the clock?" he demanded. There was no answer.

"All right," he resumed, "from now on I'm delegating in this office. I'll delegate the jobs, and then we can have some system. Can't have everybody messing things up. If you'll just do what you're told, we'll get along fine."

Delegating would have eased his load greatly. What he threatened to do was not delegating, and would have increased his load. His impulsive comments indicated that he was not mentally ready to delegate. Fortunately, he cooled off and did not act on his impulse, though some of the girls remembered the threat for several weeks.

If he had been ready really to delegate, he would have been willing to take the steps described in the balance of this chapter and in the following chapter.

Be willing to entrust responsibilities

Originally, delegating meant to entrust some affairs, usually important ones, to the care of another person.

Today, delegating includes minor affairs as well. It is not the importance of the mission, but the entrusting of part of it to another person that is delegating [8, 84, 85, 93].

For centuries the term was used mostly in connection with government, or legal activities.

The early use of delegating in business was modeled after the governmental use, and the legalistic concepts of responsibility and authority were emphasized. That emphasis had the unfortunate effect of obscuring the practical human relations involved in delegating [63, 90].

Corporation lawyers, and the older executives, still often think of delegating as a legal process, like transferring a property title. But it is not the legal charter that makes delegating click—it is people.

The key to the modern meaning of delegating is in the word *entrust*. To entrust to, or delegate to a person is (*a*) to surrender the detail to him, (*b*) with confidence in his ability to do it faithfully. Quite different from: "If you'll just do what you're told to, we'll get along fine."

The degree of delegating depends upon the amount of entrusting shown, not upon the size of the project. President Truman delegated large projects, but kept such close watch that the actual delegating was slight and did not ease his own load much. President Eisenhower delegates small as well as large projects; he gives his delegatees great freedom of decision and action within the policies of his administration, so delegating eases his burdens greatly.

Truman had had little experience in delegating when he went into office, and was a "do it yourself" man. Eisenhower had had long experience with delegating, and was more of a "get-a-capable-person-to-do-it,-and-give-him-freedom-and-support" man when he moved into the White House. This difference reminds us that delegating is almost always learned slowly, by easy stages—or that it takes time for the readiness to ripen, if it ever does ripen.

Whenever we imagine we are delegating, we should ask ourselves two questions which will show whether we are actually entrusting the detail to the other person:

1. Am I really letting him do it (surrender); or am I keeping strings attached, or criticizing him, or holding back authority, which hamper his freedom to decide and take suitable action?
2. Am I at ease about his ability to do it faithfully; or did I delegate too much too soon, or to a person I doubt may be able to do it properly?

If we don't entrust, we are assigning, not delegating. A few people seem to be temperamentally unable to cultivate this aspect of readiness for delegating—Henry Ford, for example.

The early business development of John D. Rockefeller, Jr., was speeded up by his father's entrusting attitude toward him. As a young man out of college, the younger Rockefeller signed many legal papers which had to be signed, although his father had not given definite authority. His father took this entrusting risk on transactions amounting to some seventy-five million dollars, without censuring his son for overstepping his authority [35].

Be willing to give freedom for action

Close supervision, the boss "breathing down one's neck," or restrictions on planning or doing make delegating incomplete. That is the common reason parents have poor results when they delegate household chores to children. But it is also far from rare in business and industry.

We are ready to delegate when our attitudes and temperament allow us to hand over the details to the other person to do mostly on his own, the only limits being those that are set by the policies and objectives of the enterprise.

Such a permissive attitude, with wide freedom allowed the delegates, has been the keystone of the successful decentralization (delegating) of one of the world's largest medical supply manufacturers. One instance is the freedom to plan, decide, and act, which the chairman gave the man who was sent to establish plants in South America. During this man's first three years south of the equator, the dynamic chairman "interfered" with him just twice.

Once it was a letter to congratulate him on the headway he had made the first year. The other time was a long birthday letter which contained mostly news about the home office.

It requires great self-restraint for a results-seeking executive to pass along and maintain the freedom for acting that is needed for delegating. But this self-discipline appears essential if he is to become ready to blossom as a successful delegator [85].

The leader must also be willing to take the time needed to train employees so they can be entrusted with a larger degree of freedom. The employees have to be coached by easy stages in business thinking and action before they are turned entirely loose. During this coaching period— two or more years—the executive has to be willing to accept the beginner's share of blunders, and to help the delegatees land on their feet when they do blunder [37].

Be willing to delegate to strengthen the organization

Probably the most common reason for starting to delegate is to make the executive's job easier. Although this might be looked upon as a selfish reason, it usually benefits the enterprise. Job-pressed executives deteriorate, get out of touch with new trends, slur details, get behind schedule with vital decisions, and reach superficial decisions.

But when responsibilities are delegated primarily to make it easier for the executive, the responsibilities are not always accepted with enthusiasm.

The worker's unreadiness may be due to his feeling that he is being imposed upon, or demoted to messenger boy. This is especially the case when he is not given freedom to use his own initiative to work out the detail, and is not granted authority to implement his decisions.

It is often hazardous for an executive to begin delegating just to make his job simpler. Delegating works out better when the delegatee feels he is doing things *with* the executive, or for a common goal, than when he feels that he is only doing chores *for* the executive.

That is particularly the case when dirty details are delegated. One executive passed along information about pay raises himself, but had his right-hand man convey news about layoffs, job degrading, and discipline. It is not surprising that turnover was high among his assistants, who did not relish being hatchet men and executioners.

When delegating is tackled as a professional, or leadership, problem, the chief objective is to strengthen the organization. This is almost always the reason why a firm embarks on a program of delegating, or decentralizing.

When the motivation is to strengthen the organization, the executive is ready and willing to:

1. Look for unused talents among his workers
2. Help develop those talents in directions which will strengthen the firm

The talents for strengthening the firm bear on business thinking and executive judgment. Those are hardly talents that would be developed in errand boy or hatchet-man roles.

When he is delegating to strengthen the organization, the goal is to develop men and women who can take over parts, perhaps all, of the executive's own job. This frightens some into unreadiness for delegating. They imagine they might delegate themselves out of a job, though an executive dare not be promoted until there is a replacement for him.

On this aspect, chairman Walter C. Teagle told Standard Oil Company of New Jersey executives: "No executive has done his full duty until he has made available for promotion a man capable of assuming and administering his office."

And chairman James F. Lincoln, of the Lincoln Electric Company, said: "A strong leader knows that if he develops his associates he will be even stronger."

Be willing to start by easy stages

The practical man who is in a hurry to get things done usually puts full steam into whatever he starts. Once he decides to delegate, he may make an energetic start, as Frederic H. did. But he may not actually delegate because his attitudes and expectations do not allow him to permit his employees to act for him.

Attitudes and expectations change slowly. Leaders and followers both have to be conditioned slowly to the changed responsibilities and relationships which are the heart and soul of delegating. Full steam ahead, before full readiness on both sides, is as likely to lead to a crisis as to success. In view of this, we can appreciate the soundness of some advice:

1. Take it by easy stages when starting to delegate.
2. Don't delegate more than your attitudes and expectations will allow you to pass along without too many strings attached.

Executives who are reluctant to share their responsibilities usually find it easier to give them up by degrees, a few at a time.

And those who mistrust others' judgment can gain a little more trust if they start by letting employees make decisions about little things first.

Beginners have a common failing, whatever the endeavor: they overdo. With delegating, the beginner may delegate too much and too suddenly. A small start cuts down the chances of overdoing and also gives one an opportunity to work out the "bugs" with some trial runs [39].

As in all learning, a successful start is of great importance. And the small-scale start is more likely to be suc-

cessful. It will also seem more successful to all participants
if they

1. Have reasonable expectations about what the delegatee
   can do
2. Expect him to do it his own way rather than as the
   executive might do it
3. Expect it to take some time before both executive and
   employee are satisfied with the way it is going

The strategies which some firms use to get men to delegate have forced the executives to jump in with both feet
rather than by easy stages. John R. Patterson, founder of
the National Cash Register Company, sometimes abruptly
ordered a section head to take a vacation. This gave the
section head only a few hours to start delegating his duties,
and did little to give him the state of mind that makes
delegating most effective. The Patterson "shock treatment," as it might be called, can be recommended only
as a last resort.

Other firms keep prodding executives to delegate by
easy stages. The idea of delegating is kept in the atmosphere. Harry A. DeButts, president of the Southern Rail-
way, continually asks his executives: "Who in your department would be capable of taking over your job tomorrow?"
Five of their executives have become presidents of other
companies within one year, which indicates not that they
delegated themselves out of jobs, but into better jobs.

In another company the personnel department gave
new employees instructions which prodded the production
executives into more delegating by easy stages: "Ask your
boss for the names of one or two people from whom you

can get work information when he is tied up or out of the department."

Be willing to let them make more of the decisions

Assigning chores, dirty details, or errands does not require any special readiness on the part of the executive.

The essence of delegating, however, is to pass along routine decision making so that time is released for the executive to use for making more far-reaching decisions and plans. This requires a large amount of readiness, as well as practice, especially for the executive who wants the staff to know who is boss.

As a relatively painless start, by an easy stage, the executive can *ask employees for their ideas* about problems that arise in connection with their work.

Or, when they come to the executive for some minor decision, he can *turn the question back for them to decide,* commenting that he has confidence in their ability to handle it. This is not delegating to one "crown prince," or special assistant, but to as many workers as are directly involved.

As simple as those two easy steps are, they can relieve an executive of an astonishing number of details and interruptions. Yet it is common to overlook these opportunities for minor delegating by easy stages. The account of the automobile-assembly foremen, given in Chapter 1, showed both the benefits of doing this and also the neglect that is common.

For some executives the readiness to pass along even minor decision making is difficult to come by. They feel that it would be abdicating, that it would lower their

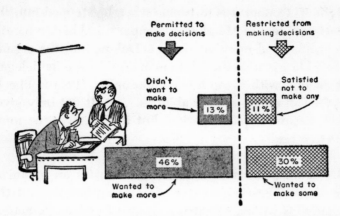

Permitted to make decisions

Restricted from making decisions

Didn't want to make more → 13%

Satisfied not to make any ← 11%

Wanted to make more ↗ 46%

Wanted to make some ↖ 30%

Three-fourths of the office clerks wanted to make more decisions about their work [81].

power over the workers, and that it might end with the workers trying to run the business [52].

When an executive feels that way about it, his willingness can sometimes be helped if he deliberately takes the risk and turns back to the employees some of the many requests he receives to make minor decisions for them.

The next step is to go into informal huddles with some of his employees from time to time and let them take part in discussions of some broader problems that arise in connection with their work.

We must be willing to let employees do what they reasonably can to help themselves handle their job problems and small decisions. This strengthens both the organization and the executive. It develops self-reliant associates who ease the executive load more in the long run than do workers who run errands but do not lift the load of executive decision making [83, 87].

John T. Conner was forty-one when he stepped into the job as president of Merck and Company and had to handle the problems of merging Sharp & Dohme into the organization. He trimmed the job to manageable size by delegating, in line with his guiding philosophy: "People like to use the full range of their abilities. . . . It not only gives them a sense of participation, but it also gives me more time to relax."

Delegating starts with thinking, not with an organization chart. The time to start delegating is not until the executive is willing to entrust, to give freedom for action, to delegate to strengthen the organization, to take it by easy stages, and to let delegatees make more decisions.

There are some times that are more favorable than others for starting to delegate. The next chapter gives an analysis of some other aspects of timing one's delegating.

8

WHEN
TO
DELEGATE

The habit of delegating

"*Who* will take care of this for you?" One president asks that question whenever one of his executives has a change in responsibilities, or undertakes some new project.

"That question prods them into the habit of delegating," he explains. "In this business we all have to delegate all we can, all the time."

Later the president asks: "*How* is that man getting along

in looking after that detail for you?" This reminds his executives not to delegate-and-forget, but rather to delegate-and-follow-through.

"We have to keep jogging our executives to delegate and to follow through, until it becomes a working habit with them," he explains. "Otherwise their delegating works out as with the bride and groom who agreed that she would make all small decisions and he would make the important ones—after twenty years he said no important decisions had been needed."

That president's comments mirror the growing opinion that the time to delegate is all the time—not merely after work piles up, but before. Two general observations give strength to the opinion that delegating should be a habitual operating procedure:

1. Executives learn to delegate by delegating—"There is no substitute for experience." Continual delegating, whether urgently called for or not, can develop skill in delegating so that it becomes almost second nature.
2. Subordinates become trained in doing and thinking, which can forestall emergencies. This point needs emphasis, as the following illustrates.

At a state-wide conference one executive reported: "It's easy to start delegating. But my problem is to make it stick. The men keep running back to me for help when they could handle it perfectly well themselves."

Follow-through and more delegating are needed to wean employees from the habit of "running to papa." Off-and-on delegating does not train workers to stand on their own feet as well as all-the-time delegating does.

Delegate when leader and followers are mentally ready

Although delegating all the time is the ideal, there are often some limitations which prevent this. In some instances the contract with the union imposes restrictions.

Most of the restrictions, however, are self-imposed, and stem from the type of person the executive happens to be. If his workers describe him as "a close supervisor," his delegating may be largely false starts. He may assign jobs and check on performance, but not share the responsibility and permit the freedom for action that real delegating calls for.

The type of persons the workers are also imposes restrictions on delegating all the time. Some subordinates are not willing to take on added responsibilities. Others are not capable. This willingness and capability may reflect company policies, as hiring "cheap help," and also the way the employees have been handled in the past, perhaps by previous employers who "took the initiative out of them."

A sales correspondent was capable, but unwilling to accept the delegations that would have prepared him for promotion to assistant sales manager. "Sure, it is a better-paying job," he agreed with the personnel interviewer, "but I have noticed that when there is a sales slump the manager and assistant are turned out, while the correspondents stay on the payroll. If you don't mind, I'll stick to my own little job."

That illustrates the effect which company policies and climate can have on willingness to accept delegating. In some situations, several months, perhaps years, have to be devoted to changing the climate before delegating is willingly accepted and zestfully carried out.

In other instances, the workers' willingness is influenced by the executive's readiness for true delegating. If only chores and errands are passed along to employees, their willingness for picking up the load will be considerably less than enthusiastic.

The time for real delegation does not arrive until leader and followers are in a frame of mind for sharing responsibility, authority, decision making, and freedom for acting.

Delegate when a new worker is added to the team

There are strategic situations that make delegating especially significant. In these situations readiness and willingness are usually stronger than usual. Two generalizations, which have few exceptions, can be made about these strategic situations:

1. An opportunity for delegating is presented whenever there is a change in processes, products, or personnel.
2. The delegating is accepted most willingly when workers have had an active part in helping plan the change.

Let's see how these generalizations apply when a new employee is added to the team. The job content for the new man can be tailored to include some delegations, within the capabilities which his record indicates he has. If he is replacing a man, the new man's job details and delegations may not be the same as his predecessor's.

There is one precaution to watch when reshuffling job content for a new worker: Don't dump all the unpopular details on the new man.

This is also a strategic time to reconsider the older employee's delegations:

1. Which older employees should be entrusted to help plan the content of the new man's job? Which should be entrusted to explain the job details (training) and company procedures (indoctrination, structuring) to the new man? How long should this sponsorship last? What sociological factors in the work team (Chapter 6) would affect this delegation? How far in the background should the executive keep, and how much freedom can he give the sponsor during this breaking-in period?

2. How can work details and delegations be realigned among the older employees? Work pressure is usually eased when a man is added. This provides some slack for delegating some of the executive's responsibilities without making workers feel they are being loaded down. A new employee is often added primarily to provide slack so that delegating some of the executive's load to older employees will be more willingly accepted.

Delegate when a subordinate leaves

When a worker is transferred, quits, or is dropped, we would expect work pressure to increase throughout the crew. But since it does not always turn out that way, this is often another strategic time to shift delegations and make new ones which will organize the team more effectively for getting things done.

Special attention can be given to changes of delegations (a) to make them better fitted to each man's capabilities and interests, and (b) to drop duplicated activities or delegations.

It is astonishing how many duplicated or unnecessary activities can be unearthed when one digs for them. By chopping these off, and by shifting delegations so that they are more in step with individual interests, it is often possible to reduce work pressure despite loss of one man.

Some executives, particularly at the lower levels, pitch in themselves and take over some of the work that was previously done by the lost man. This does not build an organization within the team, and is generally regarded as a blunder. Instead of piling duties higher on his own shoulders, the leader's function is to redelegate skillfully to the members of the team.

Quits, vacations, and absenteeism are less disruptive when delegations have been planned in advance to take care of such emergencies. Advance planning for possible redelegating gives the organization flexibility for getting things done, come what may. This reflects our earlier proposition that the executive should devote some time each day to planning and checking on his delegations. The following chapter is devoted primarily to aspects of planning delegations in advance.

Delegate when the enterprise or department is new

In the new firm, especially if it is small, delegating tends to be on a catch-as-catch-can basis. There may have been some general planning of individual responsibilities and job content at the start, but unless the delegations have been nailed down, each person is likely to pull his own job content together.

While this may result in more job interest for the individual, it often causes serious gaps in the organization.

The supervisors who pitched in to do production work themselves had mostly low-output offices [81].

Each man is likely to perform as his idea of "an all-round businessman" rather than as a pivot at his own point in the new organization. This is especially the case where the key men have not been trained in large firms which are known for their organization and administration.

Thus, overlapping and duplication of responsibilities are produced. This sets the stage for bickerings and a struggle for power between individuals. It keeps customers and others guessing about who is responsible for what.

Important functions may be skipped also. As a common example, many small new firms neglect to delegate record keeping for income-tax purposes, until they are in difficulties with the revenue bureau.

During the shakedown period at the start of a venture, executives need to give special attention to their delegating. They can be guided by five questions which need to be borne in mind continually until the enterprise is operating smoothly on the power of its own integrated organization:

1. Are all essential activities covered by delegating?
2. Is each delegation sharply defined to avoid duplication or misunderstanding?
3. Is provision made for understudies and coaching to give flexibility and depth to the organization?
4. What controls can be used to check the effectiveness of the delegating?
5. Is each delegation within the capabilities of the man, yet difficult enough to challenge him?

Promoters of new ventures are so occupied with meeting payrolls and getting customers that they may neglect those five questions. Consequently, their organizations—meaning the delegating of duties and responsibilities—grow at random. If they get into difficulties, as a large share do during their first three years, they may call in consultants to straighten things out for them. And the consultants' first recommendations usually concern the problems of delegating, which had been "left to nature."

Delegate when given new duties

When an executive is given new duties (delegated to) by his chief, the superior seldom expects the executive to take care of them personally, unless it is an assignment to a staff assistant. The superior usually expects the executive to be responsible for getting the duties done through others, and gives him freedom to work out ways and means. Our opening incident illustrated this.

As the executive takes over the new duties, he may have to redelegate some of his former duties. If the new details are of a confidential nature that cannot be redelegated, then he should redelegate some other of his responsibilities to a qualified and willing subordinate.

Unless something is redelegated when new duties are taken on, the executive may spread himself too thin to do a good job or have more work than is possible for one man to do without developing ulcers. This natural hazard is in addition to the need for developing, by delegation, a self-sufficient organization not wholly dependent upon one man.

When the executive has plans for delegating up his sleeve, a crisis is not precipitated when he is suddenly given added responsibilities. It is good "crisis insurance" to look ahead to see what other duties might be entrusted to various workers; to let these workers have some trial experience at these responsibilities as opportunities arise; to create opportunities for trial runs if they do not arise naturally.

Such planning and practice prevents last-minute panics about "How can I find time to do all this extra work." It is another example of the desirability of forming the habit of considering and reconsidering delegations every day.

Delegate when special events come up

Life in a large retail store is one special event after another. Yet the departmental buyers move serenely ahead as if they did not know about these peaks in local activity. Organization (delegating) is the answer.

The details of the special events in the department are delegated to the assistant buyer or merchandising assistant. While the assistants are enthusiastically arranging the "Back-to-School" displays and advertising, the buyer is hundreds of miles away, shrewdly buying for the "January Founder's Specials."

Special events occur in all business, though not with the regularity and impact of the department store. The application of delegation is similar, however.

There are the collections which are made throughout a firm for local charities, arrangements for the blood bank, for the dinner to honor the bowling team, for savings-bond sales. Looking after the details of such special events can divert much executive time from business activity.

Some executives delegate handling such events to their secretaries or assistants. But a wider delegating is usually possible, and produces greater benefits—strengthening the team as well as saving executive time.

Most special events can be delegated to the grass-roots level, to a committee of the workers. This kind of delegating is usually willingly accepted by the rank and file.

Delegating in this manner spreads the participation over a wide base and usually makes it more successful. It is also good for the morale of those taking part, especially when they are given due credit and honor for putting it across.

In addition, this grass-roots delegating gives the executive a valuable opportunity to size up the capabilities of some previously untried employees. Because only general supervision is needed after he starts the ball rolling with his delegating to the committee, the executive is the gainer in both time and results.

Delegate when promoted

Each move to a bigger desk calls for delegating a larger share of one's responsibilities.

What should be done about the details from the job that is left behind? On the first promotion, from production to foremanship, there is a tendency for the new foreman to keep several fingers in his old production job. But Dr. John H. Gorsuch, psychologist with the U.S. Steel Corporation, told the Society for the Advancement of Management that a man should stop doing *all* the duties of his former job on his first promotion [43].

That means that we should delegate our old job, or 98 per cent of it, to our successor on the day we leave it. This can be done with confidence if delegating has been used to build an organization and understudies that can carry on. Such use of delegating is part of the preparation for promotion.

The remaining 2 per cent, or less, of the old job can be consulting contributions—*if* the successor *asks* for them. Consulting will last only a few weeks; after that any "helpfulness" toward the former position will likely be regarded as "unnecessary interference."

That is true even when the former position is under the

promoted man's chain of command. "Unnecessary interference" can give the successor an excuse to pass the buck
when he does not perform as well as desired. He cannot be
held fully accountable for his results unless he has been
given full freedom in his position.

Great self-restraint is often needed to wean oneself from
keeping a hand in one's old job. One can't spend several
years as advertising manager, and then easily ignore the
routine in that unit when promoted to sales manager.
There is often both affection and apprehension about the
old position. A man's ego is still involved in the success of
his old office, and it seems natural for him to look in and
give them some wisdom.

Some firms have tried to lessen this complication by
making promotions to other plant locations, whenever possible. Since he had no personal contacts or ego involve-
ment in the equivalent former position at that plant, it may
be easier for him to leave his old job alone and tend to
the new.

Promotions are sometimes made across channels with
this same end in view, as well as to give the man a more
rounded experience as preparation for possible higher
responsibilities.

Delegate when retirement approaches

Retirement was probably the situation that triggered
most attempts at large-scale delegating by the middle
layer of executives in the past. They delegated as a last
resort to prepare a successor. A spurt of delegating during
the last few months in a position, however, usually leaves

much to be desired. It is somewhat similar to starting to learn to play the violin at age sixty.

The man who puts on a spurt of delegating at this final stage may have had so little practice in delegating that he is clumsy at it. An example was the one-man-controlled patent food firm that had been remarkably lucky in changing a food fad into a national habit. As years caught up with the owner, he realized he had to train a successor. For successor he picked his fourteen-year-old grandson. As a first delegation, the teen-ager had to hand out an insurance policy to each employee as the line filed past the self-conscious youth [88].

(The youth later set up his own separate business in another state, where he had freedom to decide and act. The administrators of his grandfather's estate put a banker in charge of the food business, and it is now running with delegation and success, although the basic patents have expired.)

A hazard that goes with such late delays before delegating is that one never knows what day will be the last. Most large firms try to estimate the executive gaps that will have to be filled because of retirement or other causes. Dr. John W. Riegel surveyed this situation in fifty firms. He found that the firms usually underestimated the number of executive vacancies that actually occurred [90].

Evangelists exhort people to live each day so they are prepared to meet their Maker tomorrow. That could be paraphrased for the executive: Delegate each day so that your department will be prepared if you aren't there tomorrow.

One of the most significant aspects of the timing of delegating is not to delegate until it has been carefully planned. The next chapter deals with points to consider in planning delegatings so that the plans will be right when the time is ripe.

9

EIGHT
GUIDES
FOR
PLANNING

1. *Differences between assigning and delegating*

2. *Have all essential activities covered by delegating*

3. *Have each delegation sharply defined and its objectives clear*

4. *Provide coaching and understudies*

5. *Set up controls to check the effectiveness of the delegating*

6. *Consider the man and his groups before delegating*

7. *Set the freedom for action the delegatee can be given*

8. *Be prepared for blunders*

Differences between assigning and delegating

"I've delegated John to de-gunk the sluiceway."

The boss wasn't delegating; he simply called it that because no one liked the job, and he hoped calling it a delegation would make it more acceptable to John.

Too many people imagine that delegating is nothing but razzle-dazzle used to take the sting from blunt orders. Or that it is a verbal maneuver to make a disagreeable routine appear important. Delegating is much more than using a new kind of carrot to take the place of the whip.

Almost any task can be delegated, or it can be assigned.

107

If it is delegated, it is entrusted pretty completely to the employee, and few strings are tied to him as he carries out the responsibility. A brief, and almost accurate, explanation is that we let the worker plan and run a delegated task. We decide with him the goal to reach, and he is given the least possible supervision in reaching it. Otherwise it is a sham delegation.

When it is a true delegation, and not a sham:

1. *Responsibility* is shared with the subordinate.
2. *Authority* is passed along to him to help get it done.
3. *Decision making* is shared with him, or left largely to him.
4. He is given *freedom for actions* he thinks are needed to reach the objective.

Those four signs are almost always plain in the board of directors' delegating to the president who is to operate the enterprise. How plain they are depends upon the particular firm; a few presidents have been called "messenger boys for the board."

The four signs can also be found down through the line of control, including delegating to the rank and file. Again, it depends upon the climate or philosophy in a particular organization. It is a trend of the times, however, that delegating is appearing more and more at the first level. Delegating is no longer limited principally to the higher officers [12, 54, 60, 79].

Delegating is a more involved process than assigning a job, as the four signs indicate. We can shoot from the hip when assigning, but not when delegating. On-the-spot decisions to delegate may put the leader in a hole, unless he has become so steeped in the art that he has what some have called "second sight for delegating."

For most of us, who lack this second sight, careful advance planning is in order. Experience shows that a large share of the failures in delegating are due to lack of careful planning ahead. The time to do the groping is before delegating, not afterwards.

In all our advance planning we should bear in mind that the prime purpose of delegating is to make the organization function better as an organization. The eased executive pressure which results is a by-product of considerable value in a competitive world. But the first consideration is the organization.

The organization may include the scope of the entire firm, which is usually the main concern of the directors, and the president.

Or, the organization may be limited to the narrower scope of the credit department, or customer-inquiry section. Whatever the size or scope, the objective, when delegating, is to make that region a self-maintaining organization.

The axioms which apply when planning for delegating are much the same, whether the organization affected is of wide or narrow scope. We will consider seven axioms which will provide a scaffold for structuring plans for delegating.

Have all essential activities covered by delegating

The first axiom is to have all essential activities definitely covered. It is astonishing how many are not covered in a large share of medium-sized enterprises. Many of their functions are taken care of largely by chance, because someone happens to have an interest in them or realizes they should be tended to. This has been called self-delegation, and also, delegation by default. In such instances the responsibility and authority are vague, and the freedom for action unpredictable.

Emergencies may be precipitated by such gaps, or in other cases an emergency brings the gap to attention. An unusual example was the young west coast electronic firm that was set up by scientists and engineers who had slight business experience. After a disastrous fire they discovered they had not been covered by insurance. (But they did have life insurance on the three partners, which was payable to the firm. They wondered if they should draw lots to determine which partner to shoot in order to get funds to rebuild the burned plant!)

By way of demonstration, list in a column some of the essential activities in the section of your organization which you know best. Then beside each activity write the name of the person to whom it has been definitely delegated, and who knows what his responsibility and authority are for attending to it. You are likely to find activities that are taken care of by some employee just because he has assumed the responsibility—self-delegation. And you may uncover some activities that have dual delegation.

Have each delegation sharply defined and its objectives clear

The second axiom is to have each delegation specific, and its objectives stated as tangibly as possible.

Unless a delegation is clearly defined, the opportunities

for passing the buck and working at cross-purposes are abundant. Self-delegation, or delegation by default, is usually vague and indefinite. Vagueness and poorly defined powers are a source of overlapping efforts and of bickering.

Before delegating, the objective and scope of the responsibility that is being passed along need to be spelled out in detail—not how to do the duty, but the results that are expected, whichever way the delegate chooses to do it.

"Go to department X and make yourself useful" is a prize example of muddy delegating.

"Go to department X and report on ways their scrap can be cut 10 per cent" is a sharply defined delegation with a clear objective.

Provide coaching and understudies

The third axiom is to make provision for understudies and coaching, so that flexibility and depth will be given to the organization.

The purpose of delegating is to strengthen the organization, not to give one person a proprietary interest in one corner of the business. This axiom aims for the development of alternates, deputies, and substitutes through delegating.

The executive to whom departmental operations are delegated should be authorized—even required—to redelegate as many duties as possible to various employees. This redelegation is not primarily to ease the executive's load, but to make fuller use of workers' abilities and to develop them.

In delegating to its managers, General Electric Company writes this axiom into *all* manager-position codes. President Ralph J. Cordiner told members of the Edison Electric Institute that every executive should use redelegation to develop a second team of men who are about ten years younger than the executive.

In a growing business, the delegating to understudies may be the most useful of these seven axioms. If this redelegation and coaching are done well, there will be a reserve of trained personnel to keep ahead of the expansion, and of competition.

Set up controls to check the effectiveness of the delegating

Checks of more than one kind are needed to prevent drifting away from the objective that has been delegated. The more freedom for deciding and acting that went with the delegating, the more essential it is to keep in touch with "How's it going?"

Conversely, when the executive has set up adequate controls, he will feel less constraint about giving more freedom to the delegate. But, as chairman David F. Edwards of the Saco-Lowell Shops has observed, if the controls are overemphasized, it amounts to taking away with one hand the freedom for deciding and acting that was given with the other. There is an art in balancing controls and freedom.

Some checks, however, are necessary as a part of the follow-through that needs to be planned in detail before actually delegating. This does not mean excessive red tape, however. Informal checks can be highly effective.

The checks do more than indicate how the delegate is

making out. They also reflect the skill with which the executive is coaching and developing the man.

Four kinds of checks can be set up, depending upon the situation.

1. *Statistical reports,* such as output, costs, turnover, sales collections, power used, grievances or whatever tangible records have a bearing on the objectives delegated.

Sometimes the executive keeps such figures a secret, or he lets the delegate know about them only when the delegation is going poorly. It is more effective, however, to keep the delegate fully informed of all statistical records which bear on his performance. It does not help his decision making to keep him in the dark.

Statistical reports have the merit of being more or less objective and systematic. They are usually available, and no extra expense is needed.

But these reports also have their limitations. They usually deal with last week, or last month. Conditions may change by the time the figures are compiled. And the figures may not directly reflect any of the delegate's actions or decisions. Another shortcoming of the figures is that they usually give an over-all picture and do not point to the causes of good or poor performance.

All in all, statistical reports on operations require cautious analysis before one can conclude what they show about a delegate's capabilities. Yet, because they are in tangible black-and-white, seem to have a dollars-and-cents meaning, and perhaps are even charted, they are often given more reliance as a check on delegating than is deserved.

2. *Reports by the delegate himself* are extremely useful,

though they may be biased. The bias is not always in the delegate's favor; some delegates become overcritical of their performances and need encouragement. It is important, while coaching a delegate, to be able to sense when he is expecting too much of himself, and to help him gain a more reasonable perspective.

The reports by the delegate may be given orally, during a scheduled half hour every Monday. Or, they may be written reports at longer intervals. Both kinds are sometimes used—the written "for the record," and the oral to stimulate the man to think through some of the problems he reports.

Oral reports help delegating in three ways. For one, they keep the delegate progress-minded and in cooperation with his superior; the executive has not abdicated, though he may keep in the background as an "elder statesman." For another, oral reports give the executive an opportunity to size up the man's judgment and method of tackling problems. For the third, they provide strategic moments for coaching the man without seeming to interfere with him on the job.

3. *Hearsay reports* from other employees and departments are useful, but only up to a point. These hearsay reports can give some indication of how he works with others, how he is accepted by the team, and—depending upon what was delegated—his skill in getting things done through others.

Hearsay reports should be taken with a grain of salt, however. The hearsay is usually not on as solid a ground as the statistical reports, and may be more biased than the delegate's own oral reports. Yet the hearsay cannot be entirely disregarded. The hearsay may be wrong, but it is still a part of the social atmosphere in which the delegating has to be carried out.

If the executive is eager, or blunt, about seeking hearsay reports, he may get himself, and his delegate, in a fix. The grapevine has sometimes been started when executives sought such reports. Rumors that are started in this way can be unfavorable to the delegate: "The boss seems to suspect that Frank isn't making good."

But sometimes the rumors thus started have been unfavorable to the executive: "The boss was around this morning, Frank, snooping about you."

Unless workers happen to fear the executive, he will get sufficient hearsay information merely by keeping his eyes and ears open. It is rarely necessary to use undercover agents, though it has been done.

4. *Personal contacts with the delegate* provide some of the most useful checks on "How's he doing." The oral report on Monday morning is a personal contact. But the kind we mean now are unscheduled, informal, and where he is at work. Visits—not inspections—on the job can be used for counseling, coaching, and silent checking.

An increasing number of executives are making this silent checking more pointed by using the critical-incidence method. This was developed by Dr. John C. Flanagan and his colleagues at the American Institute for Research, Pittsburgh [29, 30].

Critical incidents are not general impressions, but specific actions which have been observed by, or reported to, the executive.

They are called critical, not because they are a life-or-death matter, but because they bear on actions which have a meaning for the delegation. Many of the actions observed on the job do not have a bearing on the success of the delegation.

The critical incidents are often worthy of some counseling during the on-the-job visits, or on the Monday conference after both delegator and delegate have thought them over. The favorable incidents are acts for which the employee can be given merited praise. The unfavorable incidents are ones toward which he can have his problem solving directed.

The on-the-job visits also make it possible to catch serious blunders early. But, as we shall see, it is often better to let slight blunders pass until the delegate gets caught in their consequences.

The visits also give opportunities for prompt authorizations which may be desirable to implement his operating decisions.

These visits are one responsibility that cannot be redelegated.

Consider the man and his groups before delegating

To whom should a particular responsibility be entrusted? It is axiomatic that we have to consider not only the man, but also his groups in planning for delegating.

The capability and willingness of the employee has to be sized up in the advance planning. Any worker is capable of carrying out some kind of delegation, but it may have to be tailored to his size. For a few delegations it may be necessary to hire a man from the outside who has had special experience.

One of the best ways to learn about an employee's capabilities is to give him some minor delegations. Short-time responsibilities are often delegated primarily to test him, and these entail the least risk. He can be tried out with a variety of short-run delegations. These give the executive a chance to form a picture, based on critical incidents, of what can be delegated to a man without going beyond his depth. The worker who falls down on one type of delegation, however, may crash through gloriously when given a different type of responsibility [58].

In the advance planning then, include a series of short-run delegations as empirical tests of how far it may be possible to go with him as time goes on and experience is accumulated.

The usefulness of rotating delegations from person to person should be considered, too, as a procedure for developing the organization in depth. Care needs to be taken, however, that two people aren't delegated to the same one-man activity at the same time.

Sociological factors within the work team—the man's group—have to be considered, because delegating is strongly affected by these. Delegating also changes these sociological factors to an extent. Delegating is not an isolated personal act, but a change in the organization, however minor the change may seem to someone outside the group involved.

Gus, for example, was undeniably the most capable man in one production crew. He was delegated to reduce scrap in the section. Although the crew recognized Gus as the most capable, he was an aggressive person. In addition, he was German and an atheist, while the majority of the crew was Irish. The group did not accept Gus as one of them. The delegation set him a little above the others in the group, so they sabotaged the scrap-reduction drive.

In the advance planning, such sociological factors need to be judged. This practice may help the executive's acuteness in social sensitivity, and benefit him in other phases of his work, besides making his delegations more effective. The material in Chapter 6 will be useful for this aspect of planning for delegating.

Set the freedom for action the delegate can be given

How much freedom will be given the delegate depends not only upon his capabilities and the nature of the responsibility delegated. It also depends upon the executive's personality. A few, probably very few, executives give too much freedom; this is overdelegating. Observers believe the more likely failing is to give so little freedom that it amounts to sham delegating.

But on the trial runs some limits are advisable because of the many unknowns. There is an art in striking the proper balance. The limitations should not tie the delegate's hands. But if there are no limitations, the way is wide open for overdelegation, or disorganization rather than organization.

In the advance planning the following limitations should be decided upon:

1. The objective or goal for him to achieve
2. The amount of money he may spend without further authorization
3. Personnel to whom he may turn for assistance; this personnel should be informed, also

4. Orders he may issue, and to whom; personnel affected should be notified of this
5. Any disciplinary authority that goes with the delegation
6. In some instances, the length of time the delegation will last
7. Reports on progress he is expected to give, and when

Each of those limits should be understood by the delegate. This is often acomplished best by working them out with him, step by step. When he helps write the ticket, he not only understands it better, but is also more likely to accept the limitations willingly. It may also head his thinking more in the direction of the needs of the organization.

A large Middle Western utility, for example, had been pushing for cost reduction in office operations for several years. There were bottlenecks, in the persons of some sectional and unit heads who took their delegations in this program too passively. But after the departmental executive included his sectional and unit chiefs in the semi-annual planning of their own budgets, these chiefs became more cooperative in cost reduction [74].

In addition, the planning may be on a better foundation when the men concerned with carrying out the delegation take part in the planning. The men are closer to the firing line, and often see things which the executive may not notice from the front office.

An instance of this occurred when a superintendent called his foremen together, reminded them of the labor shortage, and said he was going to advertise for women workers. He was delegating the placement and training of the women to the foremen. Action was delayed, however, when the foremen pointed out the lack of washroom facilities for women.

"There's one trick about management that I learned early," Lamont du Pont said. "It is to surround yourself with men who know more than you do, and listen to them." Often the employees know more about some aspects of a department than the chief does.

Whatever limits are set upon the delegation, they should be presented so that they do not seem restrictive. They can be given as rules under which the game will start, with the understanding that they can be changed if it seems necessary after the game is under way. As the delegate proves his capability, the limitations can be eased greatly.

At the planning stage it usually helps if the executive has some thoughtful one-man rehearsals to practice stating the limitations so that they will be clearly understood, yet will not seem harsh. If told the limitations bluntly, or without having taken part in arriving at them, the starch may be taken out of the delegate. These rehearsals usually help the executive clarify his own thinking, which is an additional dividend.

When the delegating is fairly uniform and covers a large number of employees—as to foremen—some firms have felt it necessary to put the objectives, responsibilities, and limitations in print. In some instances the uniform delegations are included in the formal operating manual, to stabilize the practices throughout the company. Some of these, which read as if they have been written by lawyers, seem more restrictive than they probably are in practice.

For new or starting delegations, however, there are many advantages in working out the goals, limitations, and responsibilities on an informal basis with the delegates. This gives a warm climate of mutual understanding, of solving problems together—quite different from the chilly climate that goes with a legalistic book of rules [12, 14].

Be prepared for blunders

The seventh axiom is to plan the delegation so that the man can make a mistake without causing serious consequences.

Risk taking is as common in business as fleas on a dog. The risk is rather marked in the first delegation to an employee, due to the imponderables in the situation. The capabilities of the employee and the delegating skill of his executive may both be puzzling quantities.

That is why most executives favor trial runs and temporary delegations, which shorten the risks until they are sure of the ground.

It is a rare delegation, even under the most favorable of conditions, that does not produce a few mistakes. This is especially the case when enough freedom for action is granted to make it a true delegation.

Quite often, however, it is not so much a mistake that occurs, as it is an action that the executive himself would not have taken. This is not too serious: the delegate does not need to be a carbon copy of his superior; there are various ways to pack a suitcase, and one way is about as good as another.

A vital part of the art of delegating hinges upon the executive's self-restraint to permit the trial of different methods. The delegate should not be scared to death if he disagrees with his boss over methods.

It was a favorite saying of William Wrigley, Jr., that when two men in a business always agree, then one of them is unnecessary. And at a conference of company presidents at Colgate University, Lawrence A. Appley, of the American Management Association, told them: "You have to create a climate in which subordinates will not fear bringing ideas and information to you."

It is easier to maintain such a climate and keep hands off the man being tried out, if his early delegations are such that a blunder will have little more effect than help him learn by experience. The executive can then keep his shirt on, relax, and watch the subordinate learn as his fingers are burned.

Executives who have been most successful in developing delegates usually do not mention the man's minor errors (unfavorable critical incidents). This is usually deliberate, to see if the man discovers the source of the error himself, and has the ingenuity to solve it himself. And if the subordinate reports the error himself (a favorable critical incident), he gets praise for discovering it and no criticism for having made it.

The executive's objective in such a situation is to keep the delegate at ease, so he will not hold back or distort or become defensive. He is accepted as he is today, and with the feeling that within a few months his experience on the delegation will make him more valuable.

When the delegate does report a blunder, he may ask: "What should I have done instead?" Successful delegators refrain from giving a pat answer to such problems. Instead, they stimulate the man to find the answer himself, which is an important part of coaching the delegate [77].

One of the most effective techniques for handling "What should I have done" requests is to *turn back* the question by asking:

1. "What ways do you see for handling it?"
2. "Why do you think one way would have been better?"

Turning back his questions in that fashion has great value for weaning him from "running to papa" so that he can do his own problem solving on the job without adding to the executive's burden.

This technique is also useful at the higher levels. When he was president of U.S. Steel, for example, Benjamin F. Fairless said: "When the head of one of our operating companies comes to me for instructions, I generally counter by asking him questions. First thing I know, he has told me how to solve the problem himself."

As the employee's judgment improves under job experience and coaching turnbacks, there is less worry about error-proof delegating to him—less worry, in fact, about all seven of these planning axioms.

The advance planning will also have strengthened the executive's skill in the art of delegating. He may begin to show some "second sight" so that preplanning becomes less essential. And his desk will not be as covered with details that cry for his personal attention.

A part of the preplanning is to decide what responsibilities should be delegated. In the next chapter we will see what can be delegated primarily to ease the executive's burden.

10

WHAT TO DELEGATE TO SIMPLIFY AN EXECUTIVE JOB

1. Start with a position breakdown

2. Delegate details that recur

3. Delegate for personal development

Start with a position breakdown

Executive positions have a tendency to become a hash of time-consuming details. A temporary responsibility that was taken on months ago lingers on. Details that were important five years ago may no longer be needed, but have a tendency to remain in the position unless drastic action is taken to stop them. Then there are details which the executive likes, and which are included in the position although they do not help him reach the main objective.

Thus, most executive positions come to include many details which actually have low priority. These have been called "white elephants" and "sacred cows."

In view of this, it is a useful practice to walk around the job and look at it from different angles. A rethinking of the

124

position in terms of priorities can be done several times a year. During this rethinking, details can be spotted which can be delegated or dropped, and the position cut down to a manageable size.

Some people assume that a job is as unalterable as the works of a watch. But jobs are more like office furniture than a watch. The furniture can be moved around, perhaps some of it removed, and the over-all efficiency improved by the rearrangement. Most positions can be redesigned in a similar fashion, with a resultant gain in efficiency for both the individual and his section of the organization [59, Chaps. 3, 8].

A sales manager who "repackaged" his position with the aid of a position breakdown illustrates the simple way a job can be redesigned. His firm is medium-sized, and its products are sold through retailers in the central states. The firm is more than breaking even, but it has not grown during the last half-dozen years.

This sales manager's working day was long and tight. Most of it was spent "putting out fires." The only uninterrupted time for thinking over plans for the future was evenings and week ends, and by then he was usually too tired to do constructive thinking.

He had been with the firm five years. He realized he was not on top of his job, and that his frantic activity in all directions was not getting him there. There was some satisfaction with the slight increase in sales, but the sales costs were getting out of line.

So he made a systematic examination of the assorted tasks that made up his position. His guideposts were the objectives, or goals, that should be achieved in his position: Why did his position exist? Where should his actions be headed, and why?

The answers to such self-questions gave him a perspective for rethinking "What must I do myself?" and "What might be done by some of my employees?" The job objectives gave a basis for determining priorities for the job details.

He drew four columns on a sheet of paper, as in the illustration. This gave a framework for analyzing what he did on his job (details, duties, responsibilities), and why he did it (goals, objectives). The last two columns pointed his thinking toward employees who could handle, or be developed to handle, some of the lower-priority activities.

Some people prefer to use file cards for this breakdown. They write each detail or responsibility, and its reason, on a separate card. Later they sort the cards into such piles as: "What should I keep on doing," "What might as well be dropped," and "What Doran, or Scott, etc., could do for me."

The second responsibility which this sales manager listed was adjusting customer complaints. He had assumed that he had delegated this duty to Murphy when he started with the firm five years ago. But in this breakdown he found that many of the fires he had to put out each day had been set by those complaints.

Almost immediately the reason for the failure of this delegation occurred to him: he had given Murphy authority to handle only complaints that involved $10 or less. Most complaints were for larger sums, and landed on the sales manager's desk. The limited authority forced Murphy to act as a post office; he mostly routed complaints to the

BREAKDOWN OF POSITION
To locate details that
should be delegated

POSITION: Sales manager   DATE: Feb. 1957
OBJECTIVE: Increase sales of our more profitable items.

What I do	Why I do it	Employees able to do it for me now	Employees who can be trained to do it for me
1. Plan territory	Give each man a fair chance, yet a challenge	Doran	Scott James
2. Adjust customer complaints	Retain good will without losing profit	Murphy—but give him more authority	Newton Fritz
3. Weekly letter to salesmen	Keep them informed on items to push, and build enthusiasm	Scott Osgood	James Dorcas
4. Supervise field ware-housing	Service to distant customers	This is main reason our costs are up. Turn this back to manufacturing.	
5. Help plan new prod-ucts	Keep customer appeal ahead of competitors	All the above named, but better keep this under my own wing.	
6. Work up sales deals	To motivate prospects and sales force	Why not set up a committee for this?	

chief. Raising the ante—giving Murphy more authority—
would make this delegation accomplish something.

This solution was so obvious, he wondered if he was
slipping not to have hit upon it sooner. He probably wasn't
slipping, for solutions are easier to find when the problem

is put on paper. Putting it on paper, either ledger sheet or file card, gets the problem down in words and in black and white where it stands still and stares one in the face. Our thoughts do not wander away from it.

The fourth responsibility he listed—supervising field warehouses—had been inherited from his predecessor, a grasping man who had grabbed this away from manufacturing. To correct this called for a policy change which had to be worked out across channels and in the top office.

Altogether, the sales manager filled six sheets of paper and listed nearly 3 dozen responsibilities that could be easily classified as distinct job details.

He was amazed to find that not quite half of these bore directly on executive actions. He had been spending almost as much time as a sales correspondent, for example, as he had as a sales manager. He was a high-priced sales correspondent.

For about two-thirds of the job details he could find a definite objective, although not always of executive priority. Most of these goal-motivated details could be delegated, at least in part, to employees who were already on his staff and capable of handling the details. So he gradually decentralized himself by sharing his definable responsibilities with suitable employees. (When the objective is not clearly definable, it is almost impossible for delegating to be effective.)

After his years of headaches and time devoted to complaints, he now gave Murphy adequate authority. (Unless the delegate has authority to take necessary action, it isn't delegated and bounces back to roost on the executive's desk.)

For the other third of his previous on-the-job activities, he could not discover any clear objectives. He confronted himself with the fact that he had been doing many things that had no significance for his present position. Some of

(*From the booklet "The Worry-Go-Round." Courtesy of the Connecticut Mutual Life Insurance Co.*)

YES MAN!

Good old Joe! He can't say "no." There's one in every office. Everybody takes advantage of him. Then suddenly Joe has a heart attack. He's away from the office for three or four months. Yet the business goes on.

If there is a Joe in your office, show him this example of how HiTension can slowly build up such pressure that something has to give. If it hurts Joe's feelings to realize that no one is indispensable, he'll get over it. But he may never get over the damage he inflicts on himself by taking on more than he can handle.

Joe must learn to say "no." He can't take on everything.

these had had a point years before, but he had kept doing them after their usefulness was over.

An example was a weekly report on a new item that had been put out the second year he was with the firm. It was his pet, and proved successful, but the reports had been useless for the last three years. Cutting this off eased his time, and made available the clerk's time that had been spent compiling the reports.

Several such activities were uncovered—white elephants and sacred cows. A few had been started because he neglected to say "no." He abruptly dropped these tag ends, and no one missed them. His job became less of a hash and more manageable.

In the following sections we will look at other ways in which he used his position analysis to clear up some of the disorder in which his position had become enmeshed.

Delegate details that recur

Several standards can be used to isolate the responsibilities which should be delegated whenever possible. These broad principles can be given in question-and-axiom form. When they can be applied, their greatest benefits come from straightening out the hash of details which is called executive work.

The first three axioms are interlocked, and have to do with easing the pressure that is caused by too many details—and perhaps some irrelevant ones—being included in the position.

AXIOM A. "*What keeps repeating itself in my job?*" Recurring work elements can be separated from the executive's position and delegated to employees or other positions. Elements that recur can usually be handled on a routine basis and seldom require an executive level of skill.

Because familiarity has also made such parts of their jobs easy to handle, some executives are reluctant to part with them. This was the case with the sales manager's handling of customer complaints. He enjoyed doing this detail, although it added up to considerable time each day.

Axiom B. *"What minor decisions do I make most frequently?"* Routine decision making is a recurring work element which can be delegated to others who have had suitable training in the policies and procedures to aid them in reaching these decisions.

The sales manager spent about the same total time dealing with credit and collections as he did with customer complaints. For a while he pondered the desirability of turning this responsibility over to the treasurer's department. (The treasurer was eager to have it.)

The sales manager finally decided to experiment with giving the salesmen more authority to deal with credit and collections on the spot. This delegation was extended to a few salesmen at the outset, to see if it would work. He found that the men in the field made better collection records through their face-to-face contacts than he had been making through letters and telephone calls. Add to this the fact that the men enjoyed the extra importance this responsibility gave them.

As a result of this preliminary showing, the delegation and accompanying authority was given to all salesmen. From then on the sales manager received only the scattered troublesome cases, and these he usually turned directly over to the treasurer.

✓ Axiom C. *"What job details take the biggest single chunks of my time?"* Duties which require uninterrupted or long application make an executive's time schedule inflexible, and should be delegated whenever possible. Getting out monthly and other reports and preparing for and attending meetings are examples which occur in all kinds of enterprises.

It was meetings, which the gregarious sales manager enjoyed, that took his biggest single chunk of time. He started each week with a meeting of the home-office salesmen. This took from an hour to an hour-and-a-half, depending upon how wound-up he was that morning. He also spent several week-end hours planning this meeting.

When that large chunk of time loomed up on his position breakdown, he cut this meeting time to a limit of fifteen minutes. The shortened meeting was snappier, and seemed to leave the home salesmen just as pepped up as the longer ones had. Each man also had enough time released to make an extra call on customers.

Each week the sales manager had also attended a midday meeting of his service club, and on another day, the sales executives' club. He cut these to one chunk of time a week by simply attending alternate meetings. For the sales executives' meetings he missed, he delegated various bright young men from the office to attend in his place, and they gave him a written one-page report of what they learned at the meeting that he should know. These reports embarrassed him at first; the bright young men were picking up more at the meetings than he had. This is understandable: they had been given an objective of picking up all the possible useful information, while his objective had been mostly his enjoyment at meeting with the other sales executives.

His company had fallen into the habit of having many interdepartmental meetings to discuss plans and possibilities. Some of these were scheduled in advance, but in the main they were called at unexpected and interrupting times. Because the bright young men had proven useful in attending the sales executives' meetings for him, he tried delegating them to attend these company meetings in his stead.

He gave up that form of delegating, however, when the president hinted, not too subtly, that he should attend the meeting himself, and "not send a boy to do a man's work." That hint is an example that delegating has to be tempered to various winds, and not guided solely by a position breakdown. It remains an art.

Delegate for personal development

The remaining questions-and-axioms bear on redesigning a position to make it more in accord with the executive's capabilities and interests, and more fruitful in his self-development.

AXIOM D. "*What parts of my job am I least qualified to handle?*" The assortment of tasks in most executive positions call for a wider variety of skills and abilities than may be found in one individual. Delegating can be used to compensate for executive weak spots.

The brilliant idea man who was weak in making personal contacts and could not put his ideas into operation applied this axiom when he delegated the contact and selling details to a liaison man.

When we can't remake ourselves, we can remake our jobs to produce a more successful fit through delegating.

AXIOM E. *"What job details do I dislike the most?"* Details which one person does not like can be delegated to an employee who does like them. Such a delegation will not likely be successful, however, unless the delegate finds the task actually interesting or likeable.

There is often a residue of a few disliked tasks that no one enjoys and which simply have to be endured. In case they cannot be delegated, they can at least be gotten out of the way by doing them first and having the agony over with [57, Chap. 9].

AXIOM F. *"What details make me underspecialized?"* Delegating can be used to narrow the range of one's duties and permit specialization in the desired technical field. This axiom is of significance primarily for the executive who desires a technical career.

The sales manager's responsibility for field warehousing made him underspecialized. It was also a detail which he disliked, but one that manufacturing liked.

AXIOM G. *"What elements in my position make me overspecialized?"* Specialized details can be delegated to technicians so that the executive secures time to widen his activities in preparation for a broader managerial career.

Whether an individual applies this or the preceding axiom will depend upon the type of work he wants to follow ten years from now. In either case, delegating can be used to simplify his position so that the delegator provides himself with more of the kind of experience he needs for the kind of advancement he wants.

Delegating does not need to be based on guesses, or done just for the sake of delegating. As these axioms and examples show, it can be done in a systematic fashion by consciously selecting the tasks that are reserved for oneself, and delegating everything else.

A supplementary set of guides is needed when the delegating is not primarily to simplify one's own job, but rather to develop subordinates so that they lend strength and depth to the organization. The latter is the topic of the next chapter.

11

**WHAT TO
DELEGATE
TO DEVELOP
EMPLOYEES**

1. *Delegate experience and variety*

2. *Delegate "wholeness" and clear objectives*

3. *Delegate for interest and willingness*

4. *Delegate enough challenge, but not too much*

5. *Delegate a success sequence*

6. *Delegate in a climate of mutual trust*

Delegate experience and variety

The questions-and-axioms in this chapter round out those just given. The two sets do not always dovetail. Sometimes there is a conflict of interest between the executive's wish for quick results and the long-run interest of the organization. There is no pat answer when such a conflict occurs. The executive has to make the choice for himself, and then abide by the consequences. This decision cannot be delegated, though it may be strongly influenced by the policies of higher management.

AXIOM A. *"What kind of experience does this man need to develop his full value to the enterprise?"* Delegation can make employees more useful when the responsibilities that are delegated to them are chosen with the objective of adding to the skills or molding the thinking of the individual.

In a department where cost-reduction drives had failed to produce results, the worker thinking about costs changed after the informal leaders of the work group had been delegated to make continuing cost analyses of the components the department produced. That illustrates the use of this axiom to redirect the thinking of employees.

This axiom is usually applied to round out the employee, or to give him experience in "general business judgment," so that his capacity for self-direction is developed. He can then be entrusted to make more on-the-spot decisions; the need for supervision decreases, and there is less interruption for the executive.

Applications of this axiom are usually the backbone of executive-training programs. Dr. Stephen Habbe has found that company presidents regarded the varied experience provided them as the most valuable experience in training them for executive work [44].

Quite often there may not be enough varied duties in the executive's own position which can be delegated to give the variety of experience that is desirable. In such instances, suitable responsibilities can be made available by rearranging some other positions. This is sometimes done systematically by rotating job elements, or positions, from worker to worker. Automatic rotation has the merit of requiring little attention after it is set up and operating, but it has the disadvantage of not always fitting the needs of an individual [37].

AXIOM B. *"What details could be given this man to provide more variety in his position?"* Delegating is generally most effective when it adds something new to a worker's routines. If he is given nothing but more of the same old routines, he is likely to look upon it as overloading. But variety of tasks adds spice to his position [26].

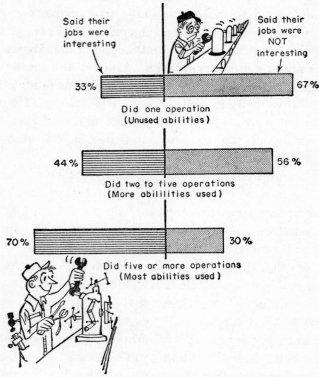

Said their jobs were interesting

Said their jobs were NOT interesting

33%   67%

Did one operation
(Unused abilities)

44%   56%

Did two to five operations
(More abililities used)

70%   30%

Did five or more operations
(Most abilities used)

(Data from Drs. Charles R. Walker and Robert H. Guest, of the Yale Institute of Human Relations.)

Job interest was greater when the auto assemblers had more variety in their jobs [105].

This axiom is superficially related to the one just given, but there is a sharp difference in the objectives. Axiom B is a corrective for the job simplification which began early this century with Taylorism and the efficiency movement [36].

The other extreme of simplification—too much variety—can also hamper an employee's usefulness, as those executives know who have too much variety in their own positions. The following axiom provides a safeguard against too much variety.

Delegate "wholeness" and clear objectives

AXIOM C. *"What could be delegated that is related to the job he is already doing?"* The delegating should produce a "job package" of tasks that fit naturally together; it should not be a catchall of odds and ends.

A machine operator's job holds together, or has "wholeness," when he is also delegated to oil and set his machine; it will lose wholeness if he is delegated bookkeeping chores, or keeping the washroom tidy.

Many skilled stenographers find they do not like a private secretary's position because of the conglomeration of tag ends which fall to a secretary. The personal aides to some men of action have a similar conglomeration of details which do not fit together naturally.

This axiom of "wholeness" is probably more important at the production line and ground layer of executives than at the higher levels [105].

AXIOM D. *"What duties can I give that will provide this man with a clear objective for him to reach?"* Delegations are carried out best when the employee has a clear understanding of what is to be accomplished and how it fits into the goals of the enterprise. Delegations are carried out least effectively when the delegate is only told what to do, how to do it, and not given a specific objective to reach by a specific time.

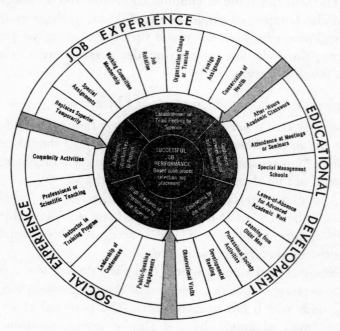

(*With suggestions by Lyndall F. Urwick.*)

Monsanto Chemical Company: methods of developing key employees.

A clear objective also does much to make a job seem whole or to give it a meaning that is not ambiguous.

The auto-assembly-line foreman tends to hundreds of odds and ends each day. But they are cemented together by the objective of keeping the line turning out 180 assemblies in eight hours.

Clear objectives thus put a job in focus within the organization, and make the responsibility for the tag ends take on some worthwhileness.

One by-product from delegating in terms of definite objectives is that the executive himself gets a sharper view of the goals that are inherent in his own position. In addition, it prevents the delegating from becoming an end in itself, and should direct the delegate's thinking more toward the enterprise and the results it needs.

Delegate for interest and willingness

AXIOM E. *"What duties would have most interest for this man, and be carried through willingly?"* The delegating should cover duties and obligations that will be accepted willingly, even enthusiastically, by the employee. The executive's enthusiasm for a task is not an index of the employee's feeling about it.

It is sometimes necessary, however, to delegate stray cats and dogs in which the worker has little intrinsic interest. In such cases, some extrinsic or artificial interest may be motivated if the delegating is made so it adds variety and wholeness to his position and gives a sharper objective.

When a detail that has low intrinsic interest for a man has to be delegated to him, special steps may be taken to add extrinsic interest. Incentives used to give prestige trappings are often useful for this. Examples are: a fancier job title, name on the worker's desk or door, no more time-clock punching, a bigger desk or work place, opportunities to talk with higher-ups (a powerful incentive, and much underused), chance to dictate to a stenographer, or a pay increase. These, in various degrees to fit a situation, may give an incentive to keep on the job, although it is expecting a great deal to imagine that they will take the full place of intrinsic interest.

Intrinsic interest may be increased by giving the delegate some inside information related to the delegated responsibility. The simplest is information about why the

(*From the booklet "The Worry-Go-Round." Courtesy of the Connecticut Mutual Life Insurance Co.*)

detail has to be done now. Or, it may deal with the profit margins on the item, competitor's moves, difficulties with sources of supply, the cost of components, and future plans which are being discussed. Such inside information is also essential for developing the employee's general business perspective and judgment.

Even when the employee does have intrinsic interest in

what is delegated to him, experience shows that delegations are executed best when the delegate is kept well informed and does not have to guess about reasons or purposes. The detail has more meaning (Axiom C) and the objective is clearer (Axiom D) when he does not have to work in the dark [59, Chaps. 7, 9].

Experiments for the Office of Naval Research, by Dr. Harold H. Kelley, have shown that simple but unfamiliar work became more interesting to workers when they were merely told it was an important job. It is not known whether the results would be similar if the delegates were familiar with the detail and knew it was actually not important, or if the work was for a long period rather than the short runs used in the tests [55].

Dr. Alan McLean, industrial psychiatrist at Cornell University, has commented in this connection: "The real problem is to make a man feel as important as he really is, by making him as important as he is capable of being" [71].

Axiom E blends with, but is distinct from, the next one listed.

Delegate enough challenge, but not too much

Axiom F. *"What can I delegate which would give him the right amount of challenge?"* A delegate develops most when a responsibility stimulates him to stretch himself to perform it adequately. Dr. Habbe found that company presidents valued such challenges in their own training [44, 68, 102].

When the delegated objective can be reached easily, the work is "baby stuff" and accomplishing it does not add appreciably to the man's level of aspiration. In addition, there may be the upsetting inference which the delegate may draw—that his chief does not think much of his abilities (that feeling of importance, again).

When simple tasks with little challenge do have to be delegated for a short span, they can sometimes be made somewhat challenging by setting a deadline for completion. This is not as true, however, for those weekly or daily quotas which are set on long-span repetitive production.

Easy work "which anyone could do" may seem more challenging if the man is told it is up to him to do the work on his own, and is given only general supervision. When asked about job experiences which had been most valuable in their development, top executives of the International Harvester Company all cited a supervisor who gave them considerable leeway in doing a job.

A touch of challenge may also be added by giving the man proportionately more authority than would ordinarily go with the detail, or more than he has been used to having. In one financial office, for example, the use of the interphone was restricted. But the use was extended to otherwise restricted clerks during the period they were working on some short-run montonous routines.

It cannot be overemphasized, however, that care needs to be exercised that the delegated duties are *not too much of a challenge*. Each new detail amounts to a man's test of himself. He wonders, "Have I got what it takes?" When the new responsibility represents too much of a challenge, it becomes a threat which baffles and frustrates him.

A delegate who feels that he has been put beyond his depth may lose his steam. Or he may blow off steam. Or he may feel butterflies in his stomach [59, Chap. 17].

A man sometimes turns down promotions because he feels the new responsibilities would be too much of a challenge.

(From the booklet "The Worry-Go-Round." Courtesy of the Connecticut Mutual Life Insurance Co.)

HAVE I GOT WHAT IT TAKES?

Every businessman will recognize this fellow. All his working life he has fought to get to the top. Now his big moment has come. Suddenly panic grips him.

HiTension is beginning to bore in, create anxieties and undermine his self-confidence. If our friend doesn't understand it's only natural to have a few momentary qualms, he's in for trouble. A mature man knows he can master his fears by facing them. When opportunities come, he accepts them gladly, takes his responsibilities in his stride.

If this man hadn't shown plenty of ability during his career, he wouldn't have been chosen for an important job. So what's he worrying about?

The problem of having enough challenge, but not too much, brings us back full circle to the view that delegating is an art. It cannot be worked out entirely by a position breakdown and axioms. The executive has to size up both the individual and the situation with care, then use his best executive judgment to plan delegating which will be an acceptable challenge—but not so much challenge that it will take the heart out of the employee.

Perhaps as good a guide as any for working out the right balance is the crisp statement Dr. Edward L. Thorndike used to summarize his experiments on the effects of successes and frustrations: "Work that is too hard is very bad, but not as bad as it might be" [103].

Delegate a success sequence

Axiom G. *"What sequence of delegations can I arrange which will give this man a series of successes?"* A delegate develops best when he is given another and more challenging responsibility as soon as he has mastered one. This is done by providing a series of occasions, or objectives, to which he can rise—a program of planned delegations in which each new objective is a bit more challenging than the preceding one. Each succeeding objective, however, is realistic in that it is possible for this particular person to reach it.

This is an application of the age-old educational principle of proceeding by easy steps: start easy, and let each step become more difficult. Thus the delegate has time to absorb one new responsibility before others are thrust on him. And he is not kept at one responsibility long after it has become routine to him. Another is added at the right time to prevent monotony and to keep up the challenge.

Professional industrial trainers call this the S.O.S. method—a Series Of Successes. This is much different from the old-fashioned philosophy that anyone can do anything if he only tries hard enough—throw him in and let him sink or swim; much different, too, from the rockbound notion that it is good to put a man up against the impossible, to "trim him down to size."

The sequence of successes builds personal confidence, and the man's skills grow on a more certain foundation. This is also related to willingness to take on new responsibilities.

When activities bring failure or reprimand, Dr. Kurt Lewin and his colleagues found that the activities become increasingly hated. And Dr. Harold B. Gerard, in experiments for the Office of Naval Research, has recently found that the more successful a person has been in group work, the more favorable his attitudes become toward taking further part in it [39, 64, 65].

Delegate in a climate of mutual trust

Application of Axiom G, more than any of the others, calls for the delegator's personal service during the delegation: a partnership, or coach-and-player relationship, between the executive and the employee [2, 3].

The employee will need encouragement from his chief: "I wasn't sure I could do it, but the boss said I could, and, by golly, I did it for him!"

More encouragement is usually needed than such obvious comments as: "Sure, you can do it if you try hard enough." Encouragement must be in the atmosphere between the executive and the employee. The employee should sense that the chief believes in him, and the belief should be encouraged in many direct and indirect ways. For example:

The chief backs him up, helps him fight the battles, and gives him adequate authority.

The chief does not haul him over the coals for a blunder, but helps him learn how to avoid such errors. The chief has a loyal belief in him despite the delegate's occasional failures.

The chief does not make decisions the delegate might make, without first talking it over with him.

The chief does not hold back secrets bearing on the work, but keeps the man informed about all factors that might affect the delegated responsibility.

The chief does not delegate someone to spy and report on the delegate.

The chief coaches him and gives him the benefits of his own experience and blunders.

The delegate will be especially sensitive to what the chief says and does. Asides, gestures, silences will be quickly interpreted as showing either belief or disbelief in the man. The delegate will get many meanings the executive did not intend to give [91].

If the chief should say, "Can you have this finished by Thursday noon?" it may be interpreted as meaning that the chief thinks he is too slow rather than that a deadline is needed for some special reason.

If the chief says, "Jones told me you had trouble with

the reciprocal setup," the man may interpret that as revealing that the chief is having him spied on.

If the executive nods when the man is proposing an idea, it may be interpreted as a "go ahead and do it" gesture.

In one instance an executive held out against promoting a delegate who others thought could manage the higher job. "The man is too nervous," the executive said. Then the personnel department had the ticklish task of pointing out to the executive that the man was jittery and on edge only when the executive was around. The presumed nervousness told as much about the way the executive had handled the delegate as it did about any nervousness in the man.

Probably the majority of delegates are awed, though not to the point of the jitters, by the chief's authority and power over them and their work. This is another factor which makes successful delegating a fine art in which some executives are much more successful than others.

The past two chapters have looked into job details and position responsibilities that can, and usually should, be delegated. There are some job responsibilities, however, which should be rarely delegated, if ever. Those will be summarized in the following chapter.

12

**WHAT
NOT
TO
DELEGATE**

1. *Hold on to executive actions*
2. *Do not delegate a duplicate of your job*
3. *Disciplinary power is a risky delegation*
4. *Keep control on policy making*
5. *Responsibility clings even if delegated*

Hold on to executive actions

Captain Miles Standish, of Plymouth Colony, is remembered by most people as the "fall guy" of Longfellow's story. The brave captain delegated something that should not have been delegated. The story may not be authentic, but it does serve to remind us that there are some details which it is prudent not to delegate.

Accumulated experience shows that some restrictions have to be imposed on what is delegated. The nature of present-day business organization sets up some dividing lines, and there are also psychological and sociological dividing lines [2, 4, 11, 101].

For instance, there are five classes of activities in a business organization which are essentially executive in nature.

150

According to the analysis by Dr. Peter F. Drucker, of the Graduate School of Business Administration at New York University, these are [25]:

1. *Set objectives* for the firm, or division, or department, or office for which the executive is responsible.
2. *Organize employees* into a team that can carry on efficiently and with least supervision and friction.
3. *Motivate and communicate* to keep employees challenged and informed, through informal but planned face-to-face contacts.
4. *Check results* and *analyze their whys* as guides to future productive actions and assembling of resources.
5. *Develop subordinates* in job skills and routine decision making so the organization becomes self-maintaining and flexible.

From the many recent studies in social psychology, a somewhat different set of fundamentally executive activities has emerged. This set does not conflict with the one just summarized; but it emphasizes the individual leadership over a group enterprise, and in terms of newly recognized social processes. From this point of view, this is the way the essentially executive activities shape up [60]:

1. *Set goals with the group,* ones which the group accepts willingly.
   "Our boss holds group confabs on work problems."
   "He asks us frequently for our ideas."
2. *Help the group reach the goals.*
   "Our boss gives us help when we need it."

"He sees that we have good equipment and materials."

3. *Coordinate the employees* for group activities.

"Our boss gives us work we are good at."

"He helps us work together smoothly."

4. *Help individuals fit into the work group.*

"Our boss made me feel at home with the crew."

"He is good at having the right people work together."

5. *Primary interest in the group, not in self.*

"Our boss will stick his neck out for us."

"He gives us credit and does not grab it for himself."

Either of those two listings of essentially executive activities provides a basis for deciding what not to delegate. Any job detail which bears fairly directly on anything on those lists has a high priority, and the executive should tend to it personally. Or, if it is partly delegated, the executive should keep in closer than usual touch with how it is going.

About the only exceptions are those rare instances where there is a co-executive, or where the activity is taken over by an executive trainee in the final stages of his training.

On the other hand, anything the executive has been doing that does not bear on the functions just listed (either list) can be delegated without fear that his job will come apart as an executive position. All nonexecutive activities should be delegated, if at all possible, for they only divert time and thought from responsibilities that are truly executive.

The truly executive actions are not only his prerogative, but he also dare not shuck them off.

Do not delegate a duplicate of your job

When something is delegated from the executive's position, the delegate may assume that he has been given a miniature of the chief's job. The delegate may do a large number of the chief's details, but the inherently executive functions should remain with the chief. There cannot usually be dual responsibility for those functions (as sometimes happens when there are inexperienced union stewards).

Duplicate responsibility leads either to dual neglect, or to double bossing. Someone has to signal which fielder should catch the ball.

Recent tests for the U.S. Air Force, by Dr. Walter R. Borg, have shown that the crew performance deteriorated when there were two leaders [6].

Owing to an inexperienced delegate's propensity to assume he has been given a miniature of his boss's job, it is usually necessary to make certain that he understands the boundaries. This can be done in a positive and nonbelittling manner by giving him some definite objectives to aim at.

If his delegation is vague—"Help me out"—it will sound like a miniature of the big job. But if it is made with a definite objective, such as "Run down the reason for those rejects, and let me know what you think we should do about them," he has a delegation with definite boundaries, and the implication is given that he has no authority to take executive action on it himself. This is positive, and does not appear to belittle him or tie his hands.

Such safeguards become less necessary as the subordinate becomes familiar with the procedures and ropes of the organization.

Duplicates of the executive's job are sometimes delegated, but such broad-scope duplications comprise only a small share of all delegations. Job duplicates are delegated only to the more experienced and capable individuals, who do share in the chief's truly executive responsibilities; an assistant superintendent, deputy auditor, or co-foreman are examples. Some firms operate smoothly with a chairman and co-chairman, though usually there is a division of responsibilties so that they do not get in each other's hair.

The majority of delegating, however, is not as assistant or deputy, but as assistant *to,* or assistant *for.* Strictly speaking, the assistant *to* covers a general aide, or roustabout; it is largely a staff rather than a line position.

The delegating that is made as assistant *for* has the advantage of pin-pointing the goal or objective. Examples are assistant for packaging, assistant for safety training, etc. Such job titles leave little room for misconceptions about the scope that is delegated to the man [92].

Disciplinary power is a risky delegation

Executives who have successful records for delegating are wary about delegating disciplinary power. They have seen many delegates get behind the eight ball and start a chain of grievances after using this power.

Before disciplinary power is delegated to a man, the executive must feel that the man can be trusted with it. Special coaching in how to use discipline—or how to avoid the need for it—is also usually in order.

A small share of executives, however, incline to duck

their disciplinary problems by delegating them to an assistant . . . such as the department head who personally passed out bonuses and good news but had an assistant do the hatchet work of discipline. In another instance, the executive usually left town to visit a branch when his assistant had a really tough discplinary problem to handle for him.

In most companies the disciplinary powers among the lower ranks have been curtailed in recent years and centered in the personnel department, or in the middle layer of executives. The modern foreman can usually do no more than report the critical incident which might call for discipline, but his recommendations may be a key factor in the higher-ups' decision.

However, employees who are given their first delegation are often not aware of the restrictions on discipline. This is especially the case with the man who imagines he is now a miniature of the boss and wants to throw his weight around to impress others.

Most delegations are of details that should not need any disciplinary authority. To be on the safe side, however, it is sound policy to make certain that the delegate understands that he is not expected to use threats or discipline while reaching the objective delegated.

Usurping disciplinary authority may become a problem when the delegate is aggressive, or long on initiative, or scrappy as a robin. Such types may need to be held down in this respect, but care needs to be exercised not to destroy their self-confidence or to arouse too much hostility toward the enterprise. When explaining the delegation to this sort, it is wise to emphasize that you trust them to get results by cooperation, teamwork, give-and-take, and patience.

All delegates, whether aggressive or timid, can profitably be coached on methods of getting things done through others without any need for disciplinary procedures.

Keep control on policy making

The greatest single relief the executive gets from delegating is from reducing the number of routine decisions he has to make. But this does not imply that he should abdicate his leadership and pass along all decision making.

Executive positions exist because there are tough problems that cannot be solved by most employees. The executive keeps the wheels turning, not by solving routine questions, but by tackling the tough ones that befuddle the workers. He can delegate all other parts of his job and still have enough policy-making decisions and planning left to keep him occupied.

Decisions which bear on the objectives of the firm, or of his bailiwick, are the leader's personal obligation. So are decisions which affect across channels, other plants of the firm, future plans, and large numbers of personnel. Whether to move the firm to Ypsilanti, to issue more stock, to change to a different price line—these are clearly policy decisions. But whether Oscar should remove burrs with a 6- or an 8-inch file is equally clearly a routine decision which Oscar should make without interrupting the executive.

The exact dividing line between decisions workers may make and those the executive must make is hazy and wide. It also varies from time to time. The cut-off point is higher when the executive has confidence in the sagacity of his workers—another reason for having enough capable employees.

The executive today seldom goes it alone in making policy decisions. He may confer freely with a wide range of employees in order to gather information on which to base policy decisions. Indeed, more executives are using some variety of employee consultation, or multiple management, for help in policy making. This is also done in the hope that it will develop some of their employees' abilities for spotting and thinking through business problems [40, 69].

The executive may delegate someone to gather the information on which to base a policy decision. He may ask for recommendations. But he can't evade accountability for the final decision. The policy that is decided upon has to rest squarely upon the shoulders of management, as modern business is organized.

It is much the same with responsibility in general; the executive can pass the buck only so far.

Responsibility clings even if delegated

Executives sometimes come to grief because they have assumed that they can delegate responsibility completely. But a delegator is in about the same position as a trustee, or a prime contractor who subcontracts parts of the job. He is still responsible for the detail, even though it is being handled by a delegate.

The executive may hold his delegate accountable to him for results. But in turn the executive's superiors hold him accountable to them. There have been instances where higher management assessed an executive to make good out of his own pocket for defalcations made by one of his delegates.

The executive doesn't side-step his over-all responsibility by passing the buck to the person he delegated to. The obligation for satisfactory performance runs directly back to the person who made the delegation. The delegator has good and sufficient reason for using judgment in selecting his delegates, for setting up checks and controls, and for coaching them carefully.

In theory, responsibility may seem to be delegated. In practice, it is shared. And if it does not work out properly, it is the executive rather than his delegate who will have to take it on the chin from his superiors.

These considerations underline the importance of careful advance planning of one's delegations before "playing for keeps." Before saying "Henry, this is your baby, take charge of it," it is essential to evaluate what to delegate, whom to delegate it to, when to delegate it, the instructions and limitations that go with the delegation, and the service and coaching that will need to be maintained until the man is able to sail smoothly with canvas unfurled.

When those plans are made, and the responsibility is clearly not an executive function and may be delegated, then delegate it on a trial basis and see how the sailing goes.

13

**THE RIGHT
PERSON TO
DELEGATE TO**

1. *Delegate to use the average worker's unused abilities*
2. *Delegate general participation in broader responsibilities*
3. *Delegate more to those who are not prepared*
4. *Delegate to overcome a weakness in the worker*
5. *Delegate to ease problem cases*
6. *Delegate to a supplier*

Delegate to use the average worker's unused abilities

"Delegating is O.K. for the man who has some high-priced assistants. But what can I delegate to my crew of unskilled workers?"

A sound answer to such a pessimistic question is: "You'd be amazed if you tried some planned delegating with them!" But that pessimistic outlook has kept some from using delegation. They note their workers' shortcomings and overlook the potentialities. Such a one-sided view misses the possibilities which a more optimistic leader would test and develop through appropriate small delegations.

Because most routine production jobs demand little from workers, the boss seldom has a chance to observe what they might be able to do if given an opportunity.

159

His estimate of their capacity is based on the amount of ability they put into an unchallenging job. Thus the average worker may be a great deal above his boss's notion of average, and may be capable of doing many more details for the boss than he realizes. This can be compared to the statement of the nearsighted, elderly lady who said her automobile would not go faster than 28 miles per hour; that was the most speed she had ever gotten out of it.

To be sure, each person has his limitations and ceilings on various abilities. It would be a risky operating theory to assume that anyone can do anything that might be delegated to him. But to believe that a person is capable of doing only the routine he has always done is an equally shaky theory to act upon [58].

Experience has shown that most, though not all, workers on unskilled or semiskilled jobs are capable of carrying out many of the details which keep their boss tied down to his treadmill.

In assembly-line production in one plant, about a third of the foremen successfully delegated such details as inspections, expediting supplies, and relief replacements. This sharing of some of the boss's responsibilities was done almost on a random basis, using the average run-of-the-plant worker, without much picking or choosing between them [106].

A production supervisor may not like to admit it, but a large share of his duties does not take much ability. Many of the duties merely take time, not mental capacity. Although the typical routine worker might not be able to do the entire supervisory job, there are many elements in the position which he can do about as well as the higher-priced boss. Record-keeping details are a clear example, and the possibility of delegating them is too often overlooked.

Dr. Naomi Stewart's reports on civilian occupational levels show that the average student in a commercial high school (the "average American") has enough general ability to make good as: stock clerk, shipping clerk, automotive parts clerk, motor vehicle dispatcher, receiving and shipping checker, toolroom keeper. Those jobs are mostly keeping records, and parts of them are crammed into most supervisory positions. Obviously, many of these record-keeping tasks could be entrusted to average high school graduates on the crew [97].

The most practical way to find out whether or not a man is capable of carrying out a particular delegation is to try him at it; you can't be sure until you try, and in many instances the results are astonishing. As quiet-voiced Henry Ford II has said: "I look on my job as choosing the right man—but you don't always find out about a man until you give him a chance."

1. The risk from possible failure can be reduced if the first delegations to a man are made self-terminating: "Wish you would check over that new machine and give me your idea about safety procedures for it."

2. Or, the first delegations may have a risk-reducing, short-time span: "Will you keep tabs on the supply of H-12 components *today*, and pry some more loose if the supply runs low?"

Production workers are more than willing to accept a share of such responsibilities. When they are given easy additional duties that are not too time-consuming, they usually follow through on them without disrupting their usual routines; there are records where routine output actually rose despite the time spent on a delegation.

Such output increases are understandable. There is almost always some slack that can be taken up in a routine job, even when workers are on piecework or bonus pay, or working against quotas. But the psychological factors, such as motivation and work enrichment, probably account for most of the increased output under these circumstances.

Psychologically, the delegated duty gives more variety to the work day and more zest for work. It gives a man a chance to use, even to show off, some of the capacities which he does not ordinarily use on his job. It gives him a challenge; the challenge from his routine work has probably worn thin long ago. In many instances there is a noticeable defrosting of the workers' attitudes; they become more team-minded, more responsible; and they may get a better understanding of the business, depending upon the nature of the delegation that has been made to them [49, 59, 60].

Delegations which make use of some of the average worker's unused abilities thus make the average worker a better investment. As John D. Rockefeller, Sr., optimistically stated: "Good management consists in showing average people how to do the work of superior people."

Something should be said about executives' unused abilities, also, especially of the middle and lower layers. If the executives do mostly record keeping, they are comparable to the nearsighted lady's car that was kept under 28 miles per hour.

Dr. John W. Riegel reports surveys of key people's unused capabilities in three firms. Committees of higher executives judged whether or not the men were at the limits of their potential, or whether they could run at more than 28 miles per hour. This is the summary [90]:

	HAD MORE POTENTIAL THAN THEIR PRESENT JOBS CALLED FOR
Company A	43% of key people
Company B	34
Company C	50

General Lucius Clay, who, as chairman, successfully reorganized the Continental Can Company, explained: "We found a lot of good talent in the middle and upper brackets, and decentralization (delegating) has helped develop them even more. The results have been amazing— the morale is extraordinarily high and there is a great deal of initiative."

Delegate general participation in broader responsibilities

Since World War II there has been a trend toward sharing some of the broader managerial problems with the workers as a group. This trend has not swept the country, but the firms in which it has been successful have almost a missionary zeal for it [2, 40, 69, 87].

Letting workers in general participate in problems of which they previously had been kept on the outside origi-nated partly from the conviction that it was the way to operate in a democracy. It has been endorsed by many researches in group dynamics which have shown better results in reaching an objective when a "town-meeting style" rather than a "dictatorial style" was used to reach decisions which affected the people throughout a group [17, 60].

An example is the machine plant that received an urgent government order which called for the quick conversion of a large section of the plant. Methods specialists were not available, so the management was forced to delegate the planning of conversion to the operators, with whatever assistance the more skilled machinists could give.

The smoothness with which the conversion was made opened management's eyes to the possibilities of wider delegating to tap the unused resources at the grass-roots level.

In a few instances the workers as a whole have been given an even larger share in phases of general management planning. A baby-products plant in New Jersey gathers the entire force, plant and office, together twice a month to hash over not only worker problems but also management problems.

The board of the Esso Standard Oil Company has authorized and urged general employee participation. In a booklet, *The Way to Work Together*, the board states: "We believe that better results come about through seeking a balance of viewpoints and through mutual sharing and solving of problems by the people affected." Esso has given their general employees a decisive part in determining action about smoking areas, work clothing, hospital plans, office layout, shifts in holidays, etc. [28].

Some production supervisors use the town-meeting style of delegating with their work groups. Problems affecting a crew are talked over with crew members, usually on an informal basis—shirt-sleeve conferences. This is not a specific delegation to one worker, but a more general sharing of the early stages of decision making, as we discussed in the preceding chapter.

The girls took to the changed work method better when they helped plan it

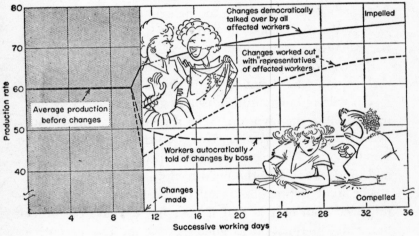

(*Data from Dr. John R. P. French, Jr.*)

Autocratic, "representative," and democratic leadership produce three distinct results when changed methods are introduced to power sewing-machine operators. All three groups were on the same piece rates, and work conditions and methods were the same.

In one metropolitan electric company, Dr. Floyd C. Mann and colleagues found that the foremen who got the best results, and were most promotable, were usually the men who "just naturally" used the town-meeting method. Absenteeism was also less under those supervisors who encouraged their men to participate from time to time in broader responsibilities connected with their work [73, 75, 76].

Delegate more to those who are not prepared

Most day-by-day delegating is of specific duties, or objectives, to individuals, not to the entire group. One's first inclination is to make the delegation to an employee who is already trained to carry it out. This is easiest on the executive—at the moment.

But the long-run wisdom of delegating to the cream of the crop only has been seriously questioned. It may overload a willing horse. And it usually generates jealousy and opposition to the favorite: "Why should I wear myself out as long as the boss always gives Fred the inside track?" In some instances it makes the "crown prince" overconfident, and he does not feel the need to develop himself further.

The most impractical result of delegating to the best-prepared man only is that it does not develop the other personnel to function as an organization. The executive becomes too dependent upon a few individuals who may be absent some days, or take other jobs, or demand pay increases as indispensable men—all the eggs in one basket.

All those hazards are avoided when one delegates to employees who are at the time not fully prepared. During the course of time, usually a short time, the executive can develop a team that has depth. This—to train and coach each man—takes more of his attention at the outset, but as one employee masters the detail, he can be delegated to take over part of the training of the next man. From then on, the executive comes out ahead in saved time. He also is getting an organization that is more flexible and useful.

There should also be less jealousy between workers, because each has had a fair chance. Any jealousies can be further allayed if the executive makes it a point to tell the employee who has not yet received any delegation that he is doing O.K., and that pretty soon there will be a duty on which he can help out the executive.

TRAINED IN NEW DUTIES — 35%

UNTRAINED FOR NEW DUTIES — 19%

Railroad laborers who had new details delegated to them tended to be higher producers, even though they realized they had little chance for promotions [53].

There is evidence that the productivity of the team may be upped as delegations are given to those who were not prepared. Railroad laborers whose foremen taught them new duties, not simply better ways to do the old routines, were more productive crews. The information in section 1 makes this increase understandable [53].

How far up the scale is it safe to delegate to those who are not prepared at the time? A 200-million-dollar financial institution in Philadelphia has the policy of purposely giving employees a little more responsibility before they have proven fully that they can handle it. In theory, this would entail considerable risk in such an enterprise. But it has worked out well enough to become a firm policy. In financial terms, the institution calls it "selling short."

The easiest way, and the safest way, is to delegate to one who is already qualified—or to go out in the market and hire someone who is, though he may have no special loyalty or ties that bind him to the enterprise. But the better method is to develop a home-grown product by suitable bits and pieces of delegation which bring out the employee's unused potentials; this brings more cream to the top.

Delegate to overcome a weakness in the worker

Delegating to overcome a worker's weakness does not always produce the personal improvement aimed for. It is usually the best way to accomplish this purpose, however. It is far superior to threats, lectures, or heart-to-heart talks.

When delegating is used *to develop a special skill* it may be helpful to tell the man tactfully why he is given that particular delegation. This gives him a personal objective in addition to the objective of the task itself.

Gene K. was an engineer who was weak in his written reports which circulated to nonengineering personnel. He admitted the shortcoming, and was keen for help. From the company library he borrowed books and articles on how to write reports. Some improvement resulted, but more was needed. He needed practice and coaching as well as reading.

Some cross-channel delegating was arranged to give him

coached experience. The sales department passed him projects. He wrote promotional folders on new items, and instructions and repair sheets for products. The projects were bona fide, not make-believe, or made work. He was producing while learning.

The needed coaching was given as he went over his draft with a seasoned writer. The engineer then revised his writing along the lines they had worked out together. After six months of this cross-channel delegating, the general verdict was favorable: "Now we can understand Gene's reports." And Gene's verdict was: "Writing reports is still hard work, but much less so than it used to be."

When the objective is *to overcome some personality weakness,* one precaution needs the greatest emphasis: *Don't* tell the man that the aim is to correct a personality fault. Clinical psychologists agree that it is useless, even hazardous, to tell a person about his personality weakness or to urge him to overcome it [59, Chaps. 16, 17, 18].

The man or woman has to discover the personality weakness for himself, perhaps the hard way, although suitable delegating can make the discovery easier. The person also has to generate his own wish to acquire a more desirable quality. Those facts are widely ignored, and with the best of intentions of helping the other person.

Thus the highest strategy is called for when setting up a delegation that is aimed to bring about a favorable change in some aspect of personality. There are three general requirements:

1. The purpose should be concealed, although eventually the employee will likely see that the delegation has been

pertinent to him personally, and he will usually be profoundly grateful for this.

2. The delegation should bring into focus the characteristic which is considered handicapping.

3. The delegation should be such that it will lead him to want to change, and also give him an objective of his own to reach.

The story of Ernie J. illustrates this use of delegation. Ernie sold a high-priced line of technical equipment, and each installation required special designing. He was the best man in the firm at adapting the equipment for the use of each customer.

But . . . he criticized prospects and customers to their faces, and he had heated arguments most of the time he talked with them. The firm kept him on only because of his design skills, and his five young children.

This state of ill will and sufferance continued until a new district manager took over. One thing the new man started was weekly sales seminars, in semi–town-meeting style. Half of each session was spent on technical problems about their equipment. The remainder was devoted to salesmanship in general.

When one of the men suggested that they talk over what to do with a customer who had a pet idea that would not work, the manager jumped at the opportunity such a topic offered Ernie. After a little discussion, the topic was pinned down to: "The relative usefulness of praise and of criticism in selling technical equipment." Ernie was delegated to lead the meeting on that topic two weeks later, "because he has such a good analytical approach to problems." (He was given flattery, not criticism.)

A couple of months later another opportunity arose to delegate a pertinent topic to Ernie: "Ways to keep from being drawn into an argument by the customer." (Notice that the blame was on the customer, not on Ernie; another good strategy.) [42].

Ernie wound up his second discussion by saying: "I never realized until I read and observed for this meeting how many traps customers set to get us into arguments. We all waste a lot of time on those arguments. Customers still make me want to straighten them out, but now it takes a really strong trap to get me into an argument with them. I have to work hard to keep out of an argument, but not as hard to make a sale any more."

Here are other examples of special delegations that were devised to lead employees to reconstruct some of their personality characteristics from the inside out:

An executive trainee who was not inclined to plan ahead was delegated to make some surveys of future possibilities and write reports on these explorations.

Another, who had the habit of jumping to conclusions, was asked to gather facts, summarize them, and then weigh the conclusions and recommend which would be the most profitable to act upon.

A lone wolf who neither gave nor received cooperation was asked to make a report on ways in which other workers were handicapped when they were poor cooperators. (Note that strategic phrase "other workers," which was face-saving to him.)

A too-cocky or conceited worker is sometimes delegated a duty which is too much for him. This is done with the hope that failing in this will "trim him down to size." In most instances, however, this merely makes the situation worse.

Delegations to overcome personality weaknesses need to be made with the fingers crossed. Many weaknesses cannot be changed, and might as well be put up with. When a weakness can't be overlooked, a direct discussion with the man is too risky to try. There is least risk, and some hope for some gain, when delegation similar to that in our examples is used.

Delegate to ease problem cases

An older sales clerk seemed to feel that her long service gave her permission to *neglect rules and procedures.* She was delegated to break in new girls, and asked to coach them especially on the rules and regulations of the store. This responsibility built up a different behavior pattern in her, and she soon fitted in better with the other workers. The fact that her sales volume increased may reflect some extra motivation that was touched off by the extra responsibility she was given.

Careless workers have been given safety delegations. Almost any comparable problem can be solved, at least in part, by a delegation that fits the problem.

In a folding-paper-box plant, teen-agers worked on a three-position operation. The three boys were full of spirit. They fooled around and joked a great deal. Their *spoilage* ran high.

The overseer delegated one of the boys to keep hourly weights of spoilage on Monday, and to reduce the spoilage as much as possible from hour to hour. Tuesday this delegation was passed to another boy, then rotated to the third, and back again through the team.

The youthful spirit which caused them to fool around made this delegation as good as a game. The rotating probably added some zest to the work, and it did cut both spoilage and pranks.

Adult *cutups* have also been toned down with delegations which give the workers some serious purpose, as well as the personal notice they crave. The sales vice-president of a watch firm delegated his problem drinker to keep the other men from overdrinking at the sales convention. It worked.

The *turnover of ambitious workers* was held down after duties were delegated to them which called for more of their abilities and enlarged their jobs. With the ambitious individual who has real potential, it is usually necessary to delegate more and more as time goes on. They are about the best capital for expanding the business.

The ambitious worker is likely to crave delegation, even to ask for it. When not given it, he has been known to develop ideas on his own, going over his executive's head with them.

The *eager beaver* is an ambitious, conscientious worker who is disparaged by others in his work group. The group often blocks the eager beaver and puts a knife in his back. Consequently, delegations that are given to him should not require the cooperation of others on his regular work team [46].

Some eager beavers are aware of this handicap and are wise enough to guide their actions accordingly. One of the noblest examples was John Adams, who, along with Thomas Jefferson, had been delegated to draft the Declaration of Independence. Adams insisted that Jefferson do it alone, because: "I am obnoxious, suspected, unpopular, and you are the reverse."

Delegate to a supplier

The buyer-seller relationship offers many opportunities for delegating when there is a climate of mutual trust. A small-scale example is the executive who telephones to a personal shopper, asking her to select and ship a birthday gift for him.

The small businessman who asks a business-form firm to design a system of forms for his enterprise is another illustration.

A druggist delegates to a supplier as he tosses his want book to the wholesaler's salesman, trusting the salesman to decide on quantities. The salesman's judgment is often better on this point, too, because he knows which items are declining in demand in the territory.

Mail-order firms delegate extensively to manufacturers. The supplier is often made a member of the team which plans products for the new catalog. The firm's merchandising skill is teamed with the supplier's designing and manufacturing skills. It amounts to free consulting services for both sides of the team [27].

Many small firms have been able to keep up with expanding markets without extra capital, by delegating to suppliers. One small power-tool firm, for instance, made

the entire tool when they started business. As the tool took
on, they were faced with inadequate facilities for keeping
up with the demand.

They decided against enlarging the plant. Instead, they
turned to others to make parts and subassemblies. They
did not buy in the open market, but set up intimate business arrangements with selected suppliers. These suppliers, now on the task force, roll up their sleeves and
work around the round table with the tool firm. Together
they hammer out plans, specifications, changes, and costs,
with no secrecy about costs on either side of the table.

The difference between this and the usual battle of wits
in the buyer-seller relationship is that this is delegating to
the supplier to help them all produce a product within a
definite price range. It is a sharing of responsibilities in
a climate of mutual trust and cooperation, with each side
coaching the other.

In the preceding chapter we learned about functions
which it is not usually wise to delegate. There are also
people to whom it is usually foolhardy to delegate. We
will learn about these in the following chapter.

14

PEOPLE WE
SHOULD *NOT*
DELEGATE TO

This chapter will be short, perhaps not sweet, but exceedingly important for the executive who is concerned about his public relations.

The habit of delegating whenever possible is a valuable executive habit. But there are instances when this habit needs to be held in check. Some of these instances are on the job. But most of them are off-the-job situations.

Executives are usually aware that they should *delegate only to subordinates.* A few less experienced executives violate this principle; so do some who are close relatives of the owner. The first promotion may also bring out some violations of this principle, in case "it goes to his head."

When a seasoned executive oversteps this rule, there is likely to be some serious reason for his slip-up.

One middle-aged executive in the middle layer, for instance, astounded his associates by making a few delegations upward, to his superiors. As he continued this upward delegating, he confided to some associate that he was actually the secret owner of the business.

That was the clue to his reverse delegations—he had developed paranoid ideas which were serious. When he was taken to the sanitarium he appraised the place, and said: "I'm glad I got here in time. They're letting it run down. I can't stand for that, because I own this, too."

In present-day business organization, the executive should delegate only to *his* subordinates, not to any subordinate. Asking another executive's secretary to do some duty is a breach of organization. It is even a bit touchy to ask another executive for permission to delegate to one of his workers. The executive asked may not object openly, but his employee will feel imposed upon and will probably mumble something about having too many bosses.

For special situations, cross-channel delegations can be worked out, as was done for Gene's report writing which was described in the preceding chapter. These usually require liaison contacts until terminated, and there will be considerable walking on eggs.

There is a further limitation on delegating to one's subordinates. The executive should delegate only to his *immediate* subordinate, not to the latter's subordinate.

In a rush for results, this is sometimes forgotten, the immediate subordinate is by-passed, and as a result actions are sometimes taken by the chief which were already provided for by the immediate subordinate. Forgetting this limitation pulls the rug out from under the immediate subordinate.

Off the job, the habit of delegating needs to be kept in the deep freeze most of the time. This may be difficult for the dynamic executives whose profession requires that they get things done through others.

One executive met a neighbor on the street and offered to give him a ride home as soon as he picked up his automobile which was being repaired. When the garage bill was presented, the executive passed it to his neighbor to check the additions, just as bills were handed to his subordinates for auditing. The neighbor took this as an imposition, and has been chilly toward the executive ever since.

Some civic-minded executives have stubbed their toes on this off-the-job limitation on delegating. They have tried to operate on community projects with the same authority they have with subordinates back in the office.

But in the civic group the executive is just another general participant in a town meeting. The usual executive habits of delegating produce the wrong results because the situation is utterly different from the well-trained business organization that is housebroken to the superior-subordinate relationship.

Some firms which were urging their executives to become more active in community projects a few years ago have recently added a footnote to this policy. They now urge executives to "take part in, but not to dominate the projects."

Now would be a good time to turn back to Chapter 3 and again study through the two lists of symptoms of underdelegating.

Then to try a hand at the project mentioned in Chapter 5—that of devising a detailed and comprehensive rating scale for use in sizing up skill at delegating.

RECOMMENDED READINGS
AND RESEARCH SOURCES

1. Anon., "Historians Rate U.S. Presidents," *Life,* Nov. 1, 1948, vol. 25, p. 65.

2. Argyris, C., "Encouraging Full Participation," *Personnel Journal,* 1953, vol. 32, pp. 50–55.

3. Argyris, C., *Executive Leadership.* New York: Harper & Brothers, 1953.

4. Barnard, C. I., *The Functions of the Executive.* Cambridge, Mass.: Harvard University Press, 1947.

5. Blum, M. L., *Industrial Psychology and Its Social Foundations.* New York: Harper & Brothers, 1956.

6. Borg, W. R., "Leadership Reactions in Situational Tests," *The American Psychologist,* 1956, vol. 2, p. 379.

7. Brooks, E., "What Successful Executives Do," *Personnel,* Nov. 1955, vol. 32, pp. 210–225.

8. Brown, A., *Organization of Industry.* Englewood Cliffs, N.J.: Prentice-Hall, Inc., 1947.

9. Browne, C. G., "Study of Executive Leadership in Business: IV. Sociometric Pattern," *Journal of Applied Psychology,* 1951, vol. 35, pp. 34–37.

10. Browne, C. G., "Communication, Supervision, and Morale," *Journal of Applied Psychology,* 1952, vol. 36, pp. 86–91.

√11. Brownrigg, W., *The Human Enterprise Process*. University, Ala.: University of Alabama Press, 1954.

12. Buchele, R. B., "Company Character and the Effectiveness of Personnel Management," *Personnel*, Jan. 1955, vol. 31, pp. 3–16.

13. Bursk, E. D. (ed.), *The Management Team*. Cambridge, Mass.: Harvard University Press, 1954.

14. Cantor, N., *Dynamics of Learning*. Buffalo, N.Y.: Foster & Stewart Publishing Corp., 1950.

15. Caplow, T., *The Sociology of Work*. Minneapolis: University of Minnesota Press, 1954.

16. Carey, H. H., "The Climate for Growth," *Advanced Management*, 1955, vol. 20, no. 9, pp. 13–17.

17. Cartwright, D., and A. Zander, *Group Dynamics*. Evanston, Ill.: Row, Peterson & Company, 1953.

18. Cattell, R. B., "New Concepts for Measuring Leadership, in Terms of Syntality," *Human Relations*, 1951, vol. 4, pp. 161–184.

19. Cohen, M. B., "Personality as a Factor in Administrative Decisions," *Psychiatry*, 1951, vol. 14, pp. 47–53.

20–21. Copeland, M. T., *The Executive at Work*. Cambridge, Mass.: Harvard University Press, 1951.

22. Dimock, M. E., *The Executive in Action*. New York: Harper & Brothers, 1945.

23. Dooher, M. J. (ed.), *The Development of Executive Talent*. New York: American Management Association, 1952.

24. Drucker, P. F., *The Concept of the Corporation*. New York: The John Day Company, Inc., 1946.

25. Drucker, P. F., *The Practice of Management*. New York: Harper & Brothers, 1954.

26. Elliott, J. D., "Increasing Office Productivity by Job En-

largement," paper to the American Management Association, Office Management Conference, New York, Oct. 1953.

27. Emmet, B., and J. E. Jeuck, *Catalogues and Counters: A History of Sears, Roebuck & Co.* Chicago: University of Chicago Press, 1950.

28. Esso Standard Oil Co., *The Way to Work Together.* Published by the company, New York, 1954.

29. Flanagan, J. C., and R. K. Burns. "The Employee Performance Record," *Harvard Business Review,* Sept.–Oct. 1955, vol. 33, pp. 95–102.

30. Flanagan, J. C. and R. B. Miller. *The Performance Record.* Chicago: Science Research Associates, 1955.

31. Fleishman, E. A., "The Description of Supervisory Behavior," *Journal of Applied Psychology,* 1953, vol. 37, pp. 1–6.

32. Fleishman, E. A., "The Measurement of Leadership Attitudes in Industry," *Journal of Applied Psychology,* 1953, vol. 37, pp. 153–158.

33. Fleishman, E. A., "Leadership Climate, Human Relations Training, and Supervisory Behavior," *Personnel Psychology,* 1953, vol. 6, pp. 205–222.

34. Fleishman, E. A., et al., *Leadership and Supervision in Industry.* Columbus: Ohio State University, 1955.

35. Fosdick, R. B., *John D. Rockefeller, Jr.: a Portrait.* New York: Harper & Brothers, 1956.

36. Friedmann, G., *Industrial Society.* Glencoe, Ill.: Free Press, 1955.

37. Fryer, D. H., et al., *Developing People in Industry.* New York: Harper & Brothers, 1956.

38. Gaudet, F. J., "Why Do They Fail?" *Business Week,* May 21, 1955, no. 1342, p. 46.

39. Gerard, H. B., "Some Factors Affecting an Individual's Estimate of His Probable Success in a Group Situation," *Journal of Abnormal and Social Psychology*, 1956, vol. 52, pp. 235–239.

40. Given, W. B., Jr., *Bottoms-up Management: People Working Together*. New York: Harper & Brothers, 1953.

41. Given, W. B., Jr., "The Engineer Goes into Management," *Harvard Business Review*, Jan.–Feb. 1955, vol. 33, no. 1, pp. 43–52.

42. Goffman, E., "On Cooling the Markout," *Psychiatry*, 1952, vol. 15, pp. 451–463.

43. Gorsuch, J. H., "Good Management Men Delegate Authority," *Advanced Management*, Sept. 1954, vol. 19, pp. 5–8.

44. Habbe, S., "Company Presidents View Executive Selection," *Management Record*, National Industrial Conference Board, April 1955, vol. 17, pp. 134–136.

45. Haire, M., *Psychology in Management*. New York: McGraw-Hill Book Company, Inc., 1956.

46. Haythorn, W., "The Influence of Individual Members on the Characteristics of Small Groups," *Journal of Abnormal and Social Psychology*, 1953, vol. 48, pp. 276–284.

47. Hemphill, J. K., *Situational Factors in Leadership*. Columbus: Ohio State University, Studies in Personnel, 1949.

48. Hemphill, J. K., *Group Dimensions: a Manual for their Measurement*. Columbus: Ohio State University, Bureau of Business Research, 1956.

49. Heron, A. R., *Why Men Work*. Stanford, Calif.: Stanford University Press, 1948.

50. Jaques, E., *The Changing Culture of a Factory*. London: Travistock Publications, 1951.

51. Jaques, E., *Measurement of Responsibility*. Cambridge, Mass.: Harvard University Press, 1956.

52. Kallejian, V. J., et al., "Managers in Transition," *Harvard Business Review*, July–Aug. 1955, vol. 33, pp. 55–64.

53. Katz, D., et al., *Productivity, Supervision and Morale among Railroad Workers*. Ann Arbor: University of Michigan Press, 1951.

54. Kaye, C., *The Effects on Organizational Goal Achievement of a Change in the Structure of Roles*. Publication 929, Ann Arbor, Mich.: Institute for Social Research, 1954.

55. Kelley, H. H., "Communication in Experimentally Created Hierarchies," *Human Relations*, 1951, vol. 4, pp. 39–56.

56. Knox, J. B., *The Sociology of Industrial Relations*. New York: Random House Inc., 1955.

57. Laird, D. A., and E. C. Laird, *The Technique of Getting Things Done*. New York: McGraw-Hill Book Company, Inc., 1947.

58. Laird, D. A., and E. C. Laird, *Sizing Up People*. New York: McGraw-Hill Book Company, Inc., 1951.

59. Laird, D. A., and E. C. Laird, *Practical Business Psychology*, 2d ed. New York: McGraw-Hill Book Company, Inc., 1956.

60. Laird, D. A., and E. C. Laird, *The New Psychology for Leadership*. New York: McGraw-Hill Book Company, Inc., 1956.

61. Lapp, C. L., "Top Management Executives Evaluate Sales Executives," *Southern Industrial Supplier*, Oct. 1955, vol. 4, pp. 4, 22.

62. Lawrence, P. R., "How to Deal with Resistance to Change," *Harvard Business Review*, May–June 1954, vol. 32, no. 3, pp. 49–57.

63. Learned, E. P., et al., *Executive Action*. Boston: Harvard Graduate School of Business Administration, 1951.

64. Lewin, K., "Field Theory and Learning," *The Psychology*

of Learning, Forty-first Yearbook of the National Society for the Study of Education, 1942, part II, pp. 215–242.

65. Lewin, K., et al., "Level of Aspiration," in J. M. Hunt, ed., *Personality and Behavior Disorders.* New York: Ronald Press, 1944, pp. 333–378.

66. Litchfield, P. W., *Industrial Voyage.* New York: Doubleday & Company, Inc., 1954.

67. Lombard, G. F. F., *Behavior in a Selling Group.* Boston: Harvard Graduate School of Business, 1955.

68. McClelland, D. C., et al., *The Achievement Motive.* New York: Appleton-Century-Crofts, Inc., 1953.

69. McCormick, C. P., *The Power of People.* New York: Harper & Brothers, 1949.

70. McKesson & Robbins, Inc., *Management-development Program.* Published by the company, New York. 1955.

71. McLean, A., "An Individual Psychiatrist Looks at Employee Communications," *Personnel Journal,* 1955, vol. 33, pp. 340–343.

72. Mace, M. L., *The Growth and Development of Executives.* Cambridge, Mass.: Harvard University Press, 1950.

73. Mann, F. C., and H. Baumgartel, *Absences and Employee Attitudes in an Electric Power Company.* Ann Arbor, Mich.: Survey Research Center, 1952.

74. Mann, F. C., and H. Baumgartel, *The Supervisor's Concern with Costs in an Electric Power Company.* Ann Arbor, Mich.: Institute for Social Research, 1953.

75. Mann, F. C., and J. Dent, *Appraisals of Supervisors and Attitudes of their Employees in an Electric Power Co.* Ann Arbor, Mich.: Institute for Social Research. 1954.

76. Mann, F. C., and J. Dent, "The Supervisor: Member of Two Organizational Families," *Harvard Business Review,* Nov.–Dec. 1954, vol. 32, no. 6, pp. 103–112.

186

77. Marks, M. R., "Problem Solving as a Function of the Situation," *Journal of Experimental Psychology*, 1951, vol. 41, pp. 74–80.

78. Maurer, H., *Great Enterprise*. New York: The Macmillan Co., 1955.

79. Miller, D. C., and W. H. Form, *Industrial Sociology*. New York: Harper & Brothers, 1951.

80. Miner, J. B., and J. E. Culver, "Some Aspects of the Executive Personality," *Journal of Applied Psychology*, 1955, vol. 39, pp. 348–353.

81. Morse, N. C., *Satisfactions in the White-collar Job*. Ann Arbor: University of Michigan Press, 1953.

82. Morse, N. C., and E. Reimer, "The Experimental Change of a Major Organizational Variable," *Journal of Abnormal and Social Psychology*, 1956, vol. 52, pp. 120–129.

83. Moser, G. V., "Consultative Management," *Management Record*, Nov. 1955, vol. 17, pp. 438–439.

84. Newman, W. N., *Administrative Action*. Englewood Cliffs, N.J.: Prentice-Hall, Inc., 1951.

85. Newman, W. H., "Overcoming Obstacles to Effective Delegation," *Management Review*, Jan. 1956, vol. 45, pp. 3–8.

86. Pastore, N., "The Role of Arbitrariness in the Frustration-Aggression Hypothesis," *Journal of Abnormal and Social Psychology*, 1952, vol. 47, pp. 728–731.

87. Planty, E. G., *Developing Management Ability*. New York: The Ronald Press Company, 1954.

88. Powell, H. B., *The Original has this Signature: W. K. Kellogg*. Engelwood Cliffs, N.J.: Prentice-Hall, Inc., 1956.

89. Reimer, E., *Creating Experimental Social Change in an Ongoing Organization*, Ann Arbor, Mich.: Survey Research Center, 1954.

90. Riegel, J. W., *Executive Development*. Ann Arbor, Mich.: University of Michigan Press, 1952.

91. Ruesch, J., and W. Kees, *Nonverbal Communication*. Berkeley, Calif.: University of California Press, 1956.

92. Sampson, R. C., *The Staff Role in Management*. New York: Harper & Brothers, 1955.

93. Seckler-Hudson, C., *Organization and Management: Theory and Practice*. Washington, D.C.: American University Press, 1955.

94. Spencer, L. M., "Ten Problems that Worry Presidents," *Harvard Business Review*, Nov.–Dec. 1955, vol. 33, no. 6, pp. 75–83.

95. Spencer, L. M., *Portrait of Company Presidents*. Chicago: Science Research Associates, 1955.

96. Spriegel, W. R., *Principles of Business Organization and Operation*. Englewood Cliffs, N.J.: Prentice-Hall, Inc., 1952.

97. Stewart, N., "A.G.C.T. Scores of Army Personnel Grouped by Occupation," *Occupations, the Vocational Guidance Journal*, 1947, vol. 26, pp. 1–37.

98. Stodgill, R. M., and C. L. Shartle, *Methods in the Study of Administrative Leadership*. Columbus: Ohio State University, Bureau of Business Research, 1955.

99. Stodgill, R. M., and C. L. Shartle, *Patterns of Administrative Performance*. Columbus: Ohio State University, Bureau of Business Research, 1956.

100. Strong, L., "Of Time and Management," *Management Review*, June 1956, vol. 45, pp. 486–493.

101. Tead, O., *The Art of Leadership*. New York: McGraw-Hill Book Company, Inc., 1935.

102. Thorndike, E. L., *The Psychology of Wants, Interests and*

Attitudes. New York: Appleton-Century-Crofts, Inc., 1935.

103. Thorndike, E. L., and E. Woodyard, "The Influence of the Relative Frequency of Success and Frustrations upon Intellectual Effort," *Journal of Educational Psychology,* 1934, vol. 25, pp. 241–250.

104. U.S. Rubber Co., *Management Development Program.* New York: Published by the company, 1953.

105. Walker, C. R., and R. H. Guest, *The Man on the Assembly Line.* Cambridge, Mass.: Harvard University Press, 1952.

106. Walker, C. R., R. H. Guest, and A. N. Turner, *The Foreman on the Assembly Line.* Cambridge, Mass.: Harvard University Press, 1956.

107. Westinghouse Electric Corp., *Management Development Personal Appraisal.* Pittsburgh: Published by the company, 1954.

108. Whyte, W. H., Jr., "How Hard Do Executives Work?" *Fortune,* Jan. 1954, vol. 49, no. 1, p. 108 ff.

109. Williamson, R. C., "Socioeconomic Factors and Marital Adjustment in an Urban Setting," *American Sociological Review,* 1954, vol. 19, pp. 213–216.

INDEX

About the Authors

Author of more than a dozen books and hundreds of magazine articles, Dr. Donald A. Laird is recognized as an authority on many aspects of business and industry. After receiving his Ph.D. degree from Iowa State University, he did further graduate study at Yale and then joined the faculty of Colgate. There he taught psychology for many years and also became director of the Colgate Psychological Research Laboratory. It was at this time that he began to turn out the books and articles which later were to consume all his time and interest. With the collaboration of Mrs. Laird he has written *Sizing Up People, Practical Sales Psychology, The New Psychology for Leadership,* all of which have had wide use among business people, business training courses, and as guides to self-improvement. Eleanor C. Laird also collaborated on *The Techniques of Delegating.*